Hero, Captain, and Stranger

ROBERT K. MARTIN

Hero, Captain, and Stranger

Male Friendship, Social Critique, and
Literary Form in the Sea Novels
of Herman Melville

THE UNIVERSITY OF NORTH CAROLINA PRESS
CHAPEL HILL AND LONDON

© 1986 The University of North Carolina Press
All rights reserved
Manufactured in the United States of America

Library of Congress Cataloging in Publication Data

Martin, Robert K., 1941–
Hero, captain, and stranger.

Includes index.
1. Melville, Herman, 1819–1891—Criticism and
interpretation. 2. Friendship in literature. 3. Men
in literature. 4. Social problems in literature.
5. Sea stories, American—History and criticism.
I. Title.
PS2388.F74M3   1986   813'.3   85-8674
ISBN 0-8078-1672-8
ISBN 0-8078-4146-3 (pbk.)

Quotations from Herman Melville's manuscript of
Typee *are reproduced by permission of the Gansevoort-Lansing Collection,*
Melville Family Additions, The New York Public Library,
Astor, Lenox and Tilden Foundations.

Design by Heidi Perov

In Memory of
Alexander Cowie
1896–1978

Contents

Contents

Preface

~~~~~~

Walt Whitman and Herman Melville were almost precise contemporaries. They share not only a common time and place but also a common vision of an America in which sexuality and politics might be joined. For Whitman the democratic potential of America lay in the realization of its homosexual potential, insofar as it could counteract the male dominance and property relationship inherent in heterosexual relations. For Whitman male comradeship was a way of combating the increasing violation of the American dream; it retained an original sense of equality and fraternity. In my work on Whitman, I found myself frequently thinking about the ways in which Melville, particularly the Melville of *Moby-Dick*, was responding to the same issues. It seemed clear to me that the male marriage of Queequeg and Ishmael was not a mere incident reflecting perhaps private sexual tastes but an essential part of a strategy for redefining American society.

Another equally important source of my interest in Melville is slightly less obvious: it derives from the Hart Crane who wrote to his friend Wilbur Underwood in June 1922, "I have lately enjoyed . . . that delightful 'Moby Dick' of Melville's including the memorable and half-exciting suggestions of dear Queequeg."[1] Four years later he wrote to Yvor Winters, "One goes back to Poe, and to Whitman—and always my beloved Melville—with renewed appreciation of what America really is, or could be."[2] *The Bridge* expressed many of the ideas that Crane had responded to so sympathetically in Melville. Like Melville, Crane constructed his major work of art around the idea of a fundamental aggressive drive in Western culture that had led to great acts of daring but had also led to the destruction of entire peoples and the suppression of the entire feminine side of culture. *The Bridge* is a love poem that concludes in a visionary recapture of Atlantis, the lost Platonic paradise. I wanted to explain to others the Melville that Crane had discovered and that I believed I knew, but whom I found so inadequately captured in the critical literature.

I share some of the cultural and political assumptions that I ascribe to Melville; it is in part for that reason, of course, that I have chosen to write about him in this way. I have endeavored to maintain a reasonable tone of neutrality throughout, however, if only to avoid standing in the way of my reader's recovery of Melville himself. But I would not be disappointed if a little bit of my own passion crept into the work: after all, a work of passionless scholarship is hardly an adequate expression of the ideas of Melville as presented here. Certain facts about American history and society need to be borne in mind. As Susan Sontag has written, "America was founded on a genocide, on the unquestioned assumption of the right of white Europeans to exterminate a resident, technologically backward, colored population in order to take over the continent."[3] In this regard America represents the last stage in the development and expansion of white European culture. That culture has permitted the regular rape of the land, which has been treated without respect or love in part because it has been perceived as property, in part because it has been perceived as woman. White European culture has regularly conquered and enslaved those of a different color—in Melville's time this process was being continued in American westward expansion, in the "conversion" of the South Seas and the conquest of Hawaii, as well as in the colonial divisions of Africa. The subordination of women by men, of colored nations by white, and of nature by law are historical facts that are related to each other and feed each other. They must be combated together. I am convinced that Melville saw these connections, that he saw the evil inherent in the social order, and that he was groping (Melvillean pun) for a solution.

It will obviously shock many readers to discover that Melville sought that answer in male friendship. What we have read about Melville has tended to downplay his radicalism—and indeed when I call him a radical I mean only that he favored substantial and immediate social change that would amount to a restructuring of society; I do not mean that he was a revolutionary or anarchist, since he rejected both of these positions. Nor do I think it is necessary that he be fully convinced of the likelihood of the changes he called for being enacted to call him a radical on the basis of his social vision. Too much Melville criticism has emphasized Melville's supposed "reasonableness," has indeed read the works as if Melville were Captain Vere. And even for those who may be prepared to consider Melville as a radical social visionary, the concept of male friendship will likely seem a poor basis for social reorganization.

Out of a desire to achieve tolerance for diverse sexualities, liberal ideology has persuaded many that sexuality is a small, private part of our lives. Such a view may be superficially true for some heterosexuals who are never required to think out the implications of their sexuality. But even then it is hardly true at the deeper level, where metaphors function. Metaphors convey truths we are frequently unaware of. When men talk about "plowing" in a sexual sense, they are revealing the deep connections our culture has established between male potency and the fertility of the land. If one is to find alternatives to such visions, it is necessary to reimagine most of our mythology. This is the task that Melville's work increasingly set itself until it reached its fullest expression in *Moby-Dick*.

Male friendship is not, of course, the only alternative to the ideology of aggressive male domination nor is it Melville's subject per se; but it is an important part of a larger movement that can ally itself to feminist and ecological thinking, as well as to movements of pacifism, political and social egalitarianism, and so forth. The male couple, as Melville imagined it, can serve as the basis for a reexamination of the way men are called upon to assume roles of power and authority. Men, even gay men, remain men, of course, and I do not blame my feminist friends who have fears about cooperation with men in the task of restructuring society. But I believe that men behave the way they do out of training and expectation, not biology; and I believe that we can all, given enough inner strength and some help from our friends, learn to be someone quite different from the men we were. After all, doesn't Ishmael?

Acknowledgments

~~~~~~

It has been a long journey, and there have been many strangers and not a few captains. I am grateful to all those who have given comfort and shelter along the way. Without them, this book would not exist.

My thoughts on Melville were first given visible (or at least audible) form in 1975, in a paper called "Melville's Vine: The Story of a Relationship" delivered at the Modern Language Association convention. In the following year I was asked by Professor Louise Habicht of Southeastern Massachusetts University to speak at a special Melville symposium that she was organizing. I am grateful to her for her support and for the helpful criticism she gave my paper. She has been a valued colleague and friend for many years. I want also to thank her colleague Robert Waxler for a sensitive critical reading of that essay.

I returned to Melville more intensely after completing a book on homosexuality in American poetry. An early version of my *Typee* chapter was delivered as a talk at the Northeast Modern Language Association and subsequently published in its journal, *Modern Language Studies*. I am grateful to the editor, David Hirsch, a friend of many years' standing, for his continued support and for permission to make use of some of the material from that essay here. An invitation to speak at an international conference sponsored by the University of Amsterdam on "homosocial arrangements" in June 1983 provided the opportunity for me to develop an essay on *Moby-Dick*, which later became the *Moby-Dick* chapter of this book. The organizers of that conference, "Among Men, Among Women," particularly Mattias Duyves and my hosts, Wim Hottentot and Frans de Rover, deserve my warmest thanks for their welcome and their encouragement. In the summer of 1983 I was fortunate to receive a fellowship from the Newberry Library to conduct most of the research for this book. I spent a delightful summer in its marvelous surroundings, not in the least daunted by the falling plaster of a major renovation project. The Newberry's resources are impressive, and its Melville collection is a national treasure. It eased my work enormously. I also received a research grant from Concordia University that permitted me to consult the newly discovered *Typee* manuscripts at the New York Public Library.

A draft of the *Moby-Dick* chapter was the basis of lectures given at Yale University and Bowdoin College, both of which provided opportunities for valuable testing of my thoughts and for useful exchange with other scholars. I am especially grateful to the organizers of these lectures who were also my hosts. At Yale University I was the guest of George Chauncey, Jr., notable historian of homosexuality, and I was also fortunate to meet a young scholar working on the pastoral and its political implications, Amitai Avi-Ram. Both of them made my stay in New Haven a pleasant and valuable one. At Bowdoin College I was the guest of Professor Joseph Litvak, whose scholarship and teaching set the highest standards. Hospitality offered by him and by Professor Lee Edelman of Tufts University provided an intellectual home and invaluable personal support.

It is not possible to remember here the many friends who have contributed to this book. I cannot, however, fail to mention my colleague Judith Scherer Herz, daily intellectual companion, nor my acute readers and critics, such as Will Aitken, Jerry Bernhard, Rudy Kikel, and Michael Lynch. Essential support was provided in difficult times by Rina Fraticelli and David McIlwraith. Special mention must also be made of Annette Niemtzow, whose studies of masculinity in American writers of the nineteenth century have been stimulating even as they have often paralleled my own work. Alfred Enns of Concordia University provided useful research assistance. The manuscript has been carefully guided by Richard Thompson through its various stages.

I must conclude in sadness and record the death of Roger Austen, pioneering gay critic. I can only express my deep regret that he cannot see this book, to whose inception he contributed.

A Note on the Text

The following Melville texts are cited in the body of the book without further annotation:

Billy Budd and Other Prose Pieces [for other prose pieces only]. Edited by Raymond W. Weaver. In *Works of Herman Melville*, Standard Edition, vol. 13, 1924; rpt. New York: Russell & Russell, 1963.

Billy Budd, Sailor: An Inside Narrative. Edited by Harrison Hayford and Merton M. Sealts, Jr. Chicago: University of Chicago Press, 1962. Citations are to the "Reading Text."

Clarel: A Poem and Pilgrimage in the Holy Land. Edited by Walter E. Bezanson. New York: Hendricks House, 1960.

Collected Poems. Edited by Howard P. Vincent. Chicago: Hendricks House, 1947.

The Confidence-Man: His Masquerade. Edited by Harrison Hayford, Hershel Parker, and G. Thomas Tanselle. Evanston and Chicago: Northwestern University Press and the Newberry Library, 1984.

Moby-Dick. Edited by Harrison Hayford and Hershel Parker. Norton Critical Edition. New York: Norton, 1967.

Omoo: A Narrative of Adventures in the South Seas. Edited by Harrison Hayford, Hershel Parker, and G. Thomas Tanselle. Evanston and Chicago: Northwestern University Press and the Newberry Library, 1968.

Piazza Tales. Edited by Egbert S. Oliver. New York: Hendricks House, Farrar Straus, 1948.

Pierre or The Ambiguities. Edited by Harrison Hayford, Hershel Parker, and G. Thomas Tanselle. Evanston and Chicago: Northwestern University Press and the Newberry Library, 1971.

Redburn: His First Voyage. Edited by Harrison Hayford, Hershel Parker, and G. Thomas Tanselle. Evanston and Chicago: Northwestern University Press and the Newberry Library, 1969.

Typee: A Peep at Polynesian Life. Edited by Harrison Hayford, Hershel

Parker, and G. Thomas Tanselle. Evanston and Chicago: Northwestern University Press and the Newberry Library, 1968.

White-Jacket or The World in a Man-of-War. Edited by Harrison Hayford, Hershel Parker, and G. Thomas Tanselle. Evanston and Chicago: Northwestern University Press and the Newberry Library, 1970.

Hero, Captain, and Stranger

Introduction

The purpose of this book is to study the significance of a controlling structural pattern through several works of Herman Melville. That pattern can be expressed most simply as the encounter of, and conflict among, three fundamental characters: the Hero, the Dark Stranger, and the Captain. It is my contention that this encounter is at the base of works otherwise as different as *Typee*, *Redburn*, *White-Jacket*, *Moby-Dick*, and *Billy Budd*. Although elements of the pattern are also present in other works by Melville, it does not dominate them in the way it does the works already mentioned, and it is for this reason that I have chosen to concentrate on these five novels, which cover a range of almost fifty years, and to deal with similar patterns in other works as part of my discussion of these core works.

Because these novels are all set at sea, this pattern of encounter is set in much higher relief. Melville also seems to be freed here from the temptations to which he sometimes succumbed in his other works either to be hopelessly prolix (as in *Mardi*) or to confuse his terms by an apparent employment of the forms of the domestic novel (as in *Pierre*). It is perhaps the fact of being at sea that gives many of their particular qualities to these works. The fluidity of the sea itself, and the absence of social norms, serves as a constant reminder of the power of the natural world and of man's very small place in it. At the same time the institution of the sailing ship, whether man-of-war or whaling ship, allows extraordinary authority to the captain, more indeed than would be available to almost any land-based authority in anything but an absolute monarchy. These facts seem to come together in the violent clash of the claims of nature and its ultimate mysteries with those of man, incarnate in the captain, and his attempt to assert authority over the ever-changing. By, for the most part, eliminating the role of women in these novels, Melville can focus on the conflict between two erotic forces: a democratic eros strikingly similar to that of Whitman, finding its highest expression in male friendship and manifested in a masturbatory sexuality reflecting the celebration of a generalized seminal power not directed toward control or production; and a hierarchical eros expressed in social forms of male power as different as whaling, factory-owning, military conquest, and heterosexual marriage as it was largely practiced in the nineteenth century, all of which indicate the transformation of primal, unformed (oceanic) sexuality into a world of pure copulation.

My concern is with the relationship between narrative and social meaning and with the consequences of this relationship for Melville's exploration of questions of literary form. My subject is not, therefore, homosexuality in itself, but the way in which sexually charged relationships between men are employed as part of a critique of power in the society that Melville depicted. This study does not search out every reference to male homosexuality in Melville's work, nor does it read all of Melville's works with equal care. Although this will inevitably lead to the slighting of some texts that other readers have found central to the Melville they have identified, it is necessary as a way of clearing the brush sufficiently so that the light of inquiry can be shed upon the subject in a new way; my attempt therefore is to look at a group of relatively well-known Melville texts from the angle of an exploration of a central structural pattern and its meanings for an understanding of Melville's larger literary and political strategies.

The meaning of this pattern of encounter I will attempt to trace in some detail in the chapters that follow. It may be useful, however, to indicate at the outset the fundamental dynamics at work. The Hero, or experiencing self of the novels, is caught between two opposing forces. One of these, represented most often by some form of the Dark Stranger—or, later, the Handsome Sailor—represents a kind of innocence or state of nature. Because of his darkness, he is, either in fact or at least symbolically, outside the world of white European civilization. His push is therefore toward natural law and against social law, a distinction that, as we will see, is crucial for Melville. The opposing force, that of the Captain, or figure of authority, represents the Western world in its search for control—control over space and over other individuals. The Captain is, both formally and symbolically, the representative of legal authority and hence the force of restraint upon the individual. The Hero finds himself caught between these two forces and obliged to choose between them. That choice is a difficult one for all of Melville's heroes, but the novels may be distinguished precisely by the degree to which the Hero is able to make the choice for the Dark Stranger and to accomplish his act of rebellion against the Captain. The encounter of these three figures, and more particularly the conflict between the Dark Stranger/Handsome Sailor and the Captain, is of special importance because of the way it embodies the conflict between two great culture myths of the Western tradition. The Dark Stranger is in effect related to the myth of the Search for the Golden Land, a myth that is fundamental to the European perception of America and hence to the American perception of itself. The Search for the Golden Land is a myth of nostalgia, a reflection of doubt at the core of "progress": for it suggests that our best hopes may lie in the past. It is a version of a Paradise Lost myth, but with the significant alteration that it presupposes the possibility of regaining Paradise. Because the Dark Stranger is linked to non-Western, and hence "primitive" cultures, he expresses in his erotic appeal the desire to return to an alternate mode of civilization. The Captain, on the other hand, is linked to the myth of the Quest for Knowledge. He is a direct descendant of Faust, who is willing to pay any price for the extension of his personal power through knowledge. As the exponent of Law and Reason, he is in constant battle with the instinctual self whose demands he must withstand. From the Renaissance explorers to the eighteenth-century philosophers, the figure of the Captain is linked to the idea of progress through civilization. In literary versions of the Faust myth, much doubt may be expressed about the role of pride in such an endeavor, but in cultural terms the myth remained potent as an expression of confidence in man's ability to improve his (and other people's) lot.

Because of these cultural reverberations of the myth, Melville was able to use his fundamental structure as a way of doing far more than giving shape to his fictions. It became a means of suggesting a dilemma that was at once personal and cultural. What gives Melville's work its exceptional force is the way it was able to capture the situation of a man, the Hero in the schema I have outlined, caught between two attractive myths. This situation was touching enough as a description of a personal plight to make his fictions work on the individual level and to make his reader sympathize with his heroes; but, perhaps more important, the situation was also one that caught the agony of a culture in search of itself. It should perhaps be remembered that the America in which Melville wrote, the America of the late 1840s and early 1850s, was one that was quickly leaving behind its own experience as a Golden Land. For one thing the rural America of the myth was rapidly being replaced by a new urban world. Melville's fictions, such as "Bartleby, the Scrivener," clearly indicate his own antipathy to the new urban world in which the values of human interchange and responsibility would be lost. At the same time, America was quickly assuming a role in international politics not so different from that of the imperial powers from which it had separated. Although Melville's own fictions do not depict American imperialism directly, their portrayal of political imperialism in the South Seas can clearly be taken as a sign of Melville's response to the imminent American betrayal of its own ostensible values. And his satire of missionaries reminds the reader of the extent to which Protestant America substituted religious imperialism for political. Underlying the entire political and cultural situation of the United States during this period was the practice of slavery, a practice that gave the lie to any American claim to moral superiority, or even to honest commitment to Christianity. By setting in opposition a *dark* stranger and a *white* captain, Melville was able to subtly remind his readers of the racism at the heart of their national life and of the need truly to embrace the values of darkness if ever the rule of "whiteness" were to be challenged.

The appeal of the Dark Stranger is not only political and mythic, it is also erotic. That this is so should not be attributed merely to Melville's personal sexuality, although that undoubtedly played a role. The Dark Stranger's erotic appeal derives in part from the way in which the figure of the Captain operates to suppress sexuality. Since the Captain speaks for the values of the mind, the Stranger is able to speak for the values of the body. Insofar as the Captain is sexual, he is a sexuality reduced to its narrowest terms: the imposition of the male on the female, perfectly mirroring the imposition of white culture on nonwhite. The Dark Stranger thus offers the possibility of an alternate sexuality, one that is less dependent upon performance and conquest. Its forms are a nonaggressive homosexuality, most characteristically manifest in figures of masturbation and idealized male friendship. Melville used his figures of the Hero and the Dark Stranger as elements in the formation of a Sacred Male Couple, whose role would be to offer a cultural counterforce to the symbols of power and aggression. Like Whitman, Melville seriously believed in the radical social potential of male homosexuality as a force in the creation of a more egalitarian society. His novels are structured around the possibility of the Hero's discovery of his own capacity for love, through love of the Dark Stranger, and the consequent discovery of the strength to oppose the rule of the Captain.

To talk about the social potential of homosexual love is to presuppose that such a thing existed in Melville's time, and I am aware that this is a point likely to be contested. Obviously, sexuality, like all forms of human behavior, is determined in large part by a social context; thus what a sexual relationship between two men *means* will vary from one place to another, or from one time to another. Nonetheless I do not believe, as some theoreticians seem to, that homosexuality was "invented" in the late nineteenth century. Melville was aware, from his earliest writings, of the possibility of homosexual relations between men; he quite rightly distinguished between homosexual practices and what we might call homosexual being, or identity. I hope my analysis will make it clear that Melville thought of his characteristic Hero as other, in large part because of his sexual attraction to people of the same sex. This otherness is one part, perhaps we might call it the negative aspect, of his sexual identity. The positive aspect lies in a sense of fraternity, a personal love that is at the same time capable of being expanded into a communal love. It appears to have been one of the greatest sadnesses of Melville's life that he was never able to find another man who could respond adequately to his desire for a love that was at once ideal and physical. That failure to translate a desire so fundamental to his thinking into a reality of his life undoubtedly lies, more than any congenital darkness of spirit, behind the gloom of his later works; it accounts for the inability of even the most positive of his fictions to do more than posit such a homosexual relation as an alternative to the dominance of a heterosexuality founded upon the inequality of partners. In part the lack of a realistic portrayal of a male couple may be laid to Melville's habitual preference for allegorical fictions, in which values are indicated rather than drawn. But it helps to explain the curious inability Melville so often experienced in ending his works adequately. In *Moby-Dick*, the work that comes closest to offering a truly positive vision of the triumph of love over hatred, poor Ishmael survives alone, only symbolically supported by Queequeg; even there, it seems, Melville was not able to imagine what it might have been like for two men to love each other *and survive*. This difficulty of imagining a life that was perforce to remain so unknown to him combined with the visionary nature of Melville's imagination and particularly of his portrayal of the basic conflict between the Dark Stranger and the Captain to create a series of works in which the nature of a truly *New* World can only be glimpsed from afar.

Readers will recognize how much my presentation of this basic structure owes to the argument of Leslie Fiedler, presented in his *Love and Death in the American Novel*. It was Fiedler who first saw the significance of the Dark Stranger in Melville's work and showed how Melville made use of what Fiedler considered a particularly American pattern of love between a white and a nonwhite male as the center of his works, especially in *Moby-Dick*. However, my own work differs from Fiedler's in several ways. In the first place, I do not locate my discussion in an attempt to identify some pattern that is particular to the *American* novel; indeed it is my view that to attempt to do so would be to conceal Melville's very remarkable achievement. I do not see as much in common between *Moby-Dick* and *Huckleberry Finn*, for instance, as Fiedler does, for it seems to me important to note the difference between the way interracial friendship works in a novel that offers a sacred marriage as its symbolic center as opposed to one that suggests only that adolescents are capable of fundamental ties of friendship untouched by adult prejudices. Putting it another way, I think one must distinguish between a novel that is homosexual at its core and one that is heterosexual at its core. The absence of sexuality in *Huckleberry Finn* is no evidence for the novel's homosexuality; similarly, it is not because of the absence of heterosexuality that one may want to term *Moby-Dick* a homosexual novel.

Fiedler's analysis is concerned above all with the sociology of the American novel; and it is coupled with a strong sense of judgment from a heterosexual point of view. As he wrote in the preface to the first edition, his subject is "the failure of the American fictionist to deal with adult heterosexual love and his consequent obsession with death, incest and innocent homosexuality."[1] The language of Fiedler's comment speaks for itself: he is studying a "failure" and a subsequent "obsession." My concern is an accomplishment—Melville's ability to find in the social and political structures of his time the basis for a radical critique that might embody the perceived need to find a place for the affection between men that Melville, and his society, required, and a permanent form to express that central concern. Fiedler's phrase "adult heterosexual love" is a telling one, since it indeed suggests that all heterosexual love is adult (and, by implication, that all homosexual love is childish, or more pertinently, adolescent). The connection between adulthood and heterosexuality may have its origins in Greek concepts of homosexuality, in which it is expected that the ephebe will, on coming of age, himself marry and assume a family, as will another ephebe in turn. But in modern discourse the concept owes far more to psychoanalysis. Here the most important text is Erik Erikson's *Childhood and Society*,[2] which imposes on Freud's notion of childhood development a grid of "stages" that insure that any deviation from the straight line toward "heterosexual mutuality" is seen as aberration, that any "solution" other than the ideal heterosexual couple is the result of arrested development. It is necessary to free our discussion of the role of homosexuality in Melville's work from such normative patterns, disguised as science, so that we can respond without prejudgments. It is surely time to recognize that many lives, in many different circumstances, will take alternate patterns from those termed normal.

The Eriksonian argument, like that of Fiedler, is founded on personal psychology. The individual is examined, and then his patterns are writ large. This procedure, which underlies the historical development of psychology as a mode of discourse, helps to explain its normative predispositions. Since only a single individual can be chosen as the type, his patterns will necessarily be invested with the weight of universal authority. But the role of sexuality in Melville's work is, most characteristically, developed in political terms and not personal ones (the—only apparent—exception to this principle is of course *Pierre*). Fiedler's greatest weakness lies in his failure to see, or to explore, the political implications of sexuality. At least once he briefly refers to the possibility of a political significance, correctly linking the sexual transgression, homosexuality, to the racial transgression. "Whatever the symbolic necessities," he writes, "which demand that the male *hierogamos* be inter-racial as well as homoerotic, that marriage takes on, by virtue of crossing conventional color lines, a sociological significance as well as a psychological and metaphysical one."[3] But the point is not developed, since Fiedler is not primarily interested in the sacred marriage as an alternative to dominant social patterns but rather as an evasion of them. It seems clear as well that Fiedler was not able to see that a homosexual union might itself, whether or not it crossed racial lines, pose political and social issues. Fiedler's book has had enormous importance over the almost twenty-five years since it was first published, and it is in fact unlikely that I should be writing the present study had it not led the way for such discussions of sexuality. But recognizing my own substantial debt to Fiedler's work, and to his identification of a homosexual strain in American literature in general and in Melville in particular, cannot prevent me from saying at the same time how painful it has been to see homosexuals' lives and artistic creations so abused, so turned to other purposes, so insistently read as failed versions of something else. *Love and Death* was important for gay people in the same way that the Kinsey Report was; it announced that we were there. At the same time, though, it instantly imposed the medical/scientific model which said, in effect, that we must be cured, just as American literature was to come to its senses and to create mature heterosexual novels.

If, thanks in large part to Fiedler, there has been considerable mention made in Melville criticism of the role of homosexuality (although no attempt to evaluate that role by anyone other than Fiedler), there has been surprisingly little attention paid to what I am calling the political implications of Melville's work.[4] By political I do not mean, of course, how Melville voted or even his precise views on specific issues of his day; instead I refer to his analysis of power and its operation. I take Melville to have been almost unique among nineteenth-century American men, aside from Whitman, in recognizing the links between sexuality and structures of power. Such a recognition is fundamental to much feminist thinking, of course, and it is striking how much Melville's work, from a male stand-point, parallels the thinking of contemporary feminists, such as Margaret Fuller,[5] even though Melville himself was little aware of their work, appar-ently, and generally unfamiliar with intellectual women of other than the most sentimental school. In more general terms, Melville used his works as a constant protest against the abuse of power. Indeed he seems to have believed that power contained the impulse to abuse, so that the only protection against its misuse was its elimination and replacement by a system of shared responsibilities under a rule of love. Over and over again the novels illustrate that the arbitrary rule of the Captain over his ship is a violation of American democratic principles as well as of the ostensible principles of Christianity (the allegories of *Mardi* make the failure of Christianity's religion of love even more explicit). One of the finest critics of American literature, F. O. Matthiessen, a person deeply sensitive to issues of power and human responsibility, connects Melville's critique of power with his response to American Transcendentalism: Captain Ahab, he says, "provided an ominous glimpse of what was the result when the Emersonian will to virtue became in less innocent natures the will to conquest."[6] It must be remembered that Melville's clear rejection of Emer-son and Transcendentalism in *Moby-Dick* (as well as in *Mardi* and else-where) does not necessarily make him a deep pessimist. Far too much has been written about the "tragic vision" of Melville in a way that has pre-vented us from seeing that the destructive drive of modern man was countered by the potential, at least, of an alternative vision; the tragedy arises only from the failure of that alternative to be realized. One of the finest statements of the issue, again specifically considering *Moby-Dick* but in many ways applicable to all the works under discussion here, is David Hirsch's remark that "one of the great achievements of *Moby-Dick*, one too seldom recognized, is the intensity with which it explores both the 're-ality' of nineteenth-century democratic man and the possibilities of the democratic dream which underlay that 'reality'."[7] Indeed Melville is a realist, as Emerson and Thoreau never were, about the conditions of life for "the people" in his purportedly democratic society. But, through the writing of *Moby-Dick* at least, he never abandoned his sense of hope for the fulfillment of the democratic dream. Like Whitman, whose work he gives no indication of having known, Melville used the male couple as a figure of an inherently democratic union of equals which could serve as the basis for a new social organization. While rejecting the individualism of Emerson, Melville did not (at least until after 1851) turn to a pessimism that doubted all possibility of human progress because of man's inability to love; instead he established fraternity as the alternative to egotism. By making fraternity at once erotic and social, he recognized its fullest potential; but at the same time he insured that his ideas would receive a mystified reception from those who are still unable to see how "sperm-squeezing" may be an act of social revolution as well as the site of pleasure.

Akin to Melville's startling link between sexual power structures and social organization is his association of questions of literary form with social and sexual questions. As Whitman was striving for the creation of a democratic poetics, one of inclusiveness, equality, multiplicity, parallelism, that would correspond to the vastness and variety of the American nation, Melville too was revising the notions of literary form and discovering for himself a form adequate to his material. One need only look at *Moby-Dick* alongside *The Scarlet Letter* to realize the magnitude of his accomplishment: against a work in its formal attributes conservative, conventional, even old-fashioned, we discover a work that breaks all boundaries of genre in its celebration of its own diverse energies. Like Whitman, Melville "permit[s] to speak at every hazard, / Nature without check with original energy." By a constantly shifting perspective best achieved in *Moby-Dick*, Melville put into question the epistemology at the heart of narrative structure. Ahab's language is another reflection of his intrusive sexuality and aggressive politics. If Ishmael, taught by Queequeg, is to bring about any change, it must include a questioning of that linguistic order that privileges meaning over the words in themselves, with their erotic surfaces fully alert. As Roland Barthes writes in that wonderful passage that concludes *Le Plaisir du Texte*, evoking his "texte paradisiaque," "ça granule, ça grésille, ça caresse, ça rape, ça coupe: ça jouit."[8]

Melville thus works toward a narrative structure that gives full recognition to the role of perception in experience and that questions the drive to know as part of an entire program of acquisitive knowledge. Only a text supple enough to reflect the various languages, experiences, and attitudes of all the participants can even begin to do justice to the presumed event that lies at its basis, like the doubloon nailed to the masthead. And language itself is set on the path to the recovery of its full tactile possibility. Surely no one can read Melville without rejoicing in the verbal exuberance, in the sheer delight of handling words, of touching them, of rolling them around in the mouth, almost as if they were the globules of sperm in the hands of Ishmael and his crewmates. Melville's language and verbal structures are at the heart of a poetics that is at once democratic and masturbatory.

A Note on the Use of the Term "Homosexual"

Some readers may object to my use of this word, which was only invented in 1869, in discussing works written twenty years earlier. They hold, in effect, that the invention of the word makes the concept possible. It seems to me quite likely that the opposite is true: the word is invented to correspond to a social reality. It is certainly true that the word, once invented and entered into common usage, has an effect on behavior. Much recent feminist scholarship, for instance, has shown how the conceptualization of the "lesbian" in the early twentieth century prevented the open display of affection between women that had previously been permissible. To some extent, the same thing is true of male friendships and affection: the widespread familiarity with the idea of homosexuality brought an end to many spontaneous forms of open affection that had previously seemed normal. Carroll Smith-Rosenberg's well-known comment about female friendships could almost as well serve as a description of the changing situation with regard to male friendships:

> nineteenth-century American society did not taboo close female
> relationships but rather recognized them as a socially viable form
> of human contact—and, as such, acceptable throughout a wom-
> an's life. Indeed it was not these homosocial ties that were inhib-
> ited but rather heterosexual leanings. While closeness, freedom
> of emotional expression, and uninhibited physical contact char-
> acterized women's relationships with each other, the opposite
> was frequently true of male-female relationships.[9]

In other words, homosocial relationships were encouraged as a way of preventing heterosexual ones, or simply sexual relationships *tout court*, it being rather innocently assumed that sexual relations were necessarily heterosexual. The same phenomenon is true of all-male institutions such as boarding schools, colleges, or the military: the exclusion of women and, to some extent, the encouragement of emotional attachments between men are designed to eliminate sexuality.

The term "homosocial" might seem to some readers a desirable alternative to "homosexual" when talking about Melville or his work (the fact that this term is an even more recent invention does not seem to bother anyone). However, the term, a linguistic monster, seems to me best reserved, if at all, for institutions and situations. Thus prisons may be said to be homosocial institutions, but prisoners remain heterosexual or homosexual, according to their principal sexual orientation, regardless of the sexual activity they may engage in while in a homosocial environment. The most serious objection to the use of the term "homosexual" comes from its apparent connection with sexual, that is, genital, behavior. In the first place, this is a misunderstanding of the origins of the term: the adjective "homosexual" refers to same-sex, or all-male or all-female. It indicates nothing about sexual activity. In common speech, however, and when the term is used as a noun, it implies sexual preference or orientation, but not necessarily sexual activity. It is particularly odd to observe that the term "heterosexual" can apparently be used whether or not actual sexual contact takes place; but a narrower definition is usually imposed on the term "homosexual." Thus if I say that Melville expresses homosexual feelings, I am referring to desires and not practices. The great majority of people who feel themselves to be predominantly homosexual encounter such feelings long before they may encounter any practices (and some may never translate these feelings into acts); conversely many people engage in homosexual practices without ever feeling themselves to be homosexual.

It would be possible, of course, to use the term "gay" to describe Melville or his characters, but here the sense of anachronism seems to me far too strong. I believe that the term "gay" as it is now used refers to a whole complex of behavior and attitudes. Important among them are the contemporary ideology of gay oppression and the concept of the gay person as a victim of ethnic or racial discrimination. While there is some evidence of such a concept in Melville, it is almost always linked to effeminacy, and effeminacy is by no means necessarily homosexual. In my opinion the proper model for an analysis of the condition of the homosexual is not the racial one but the sexual one: the situation of homosexuals in contemporary society is related to the situation of women. This seems to have been true in most times and places: even in Greece where homosexual relations were institutionalized, the person who preferred homosexual relations, especially the person who liked to be the so-called "passive" partner, was associated with women and slaves. Since it seems impossible to use the term "gay" without at least implying some late twentieth-century attitudes, I will not make use of it in the body of my argument. However, I would not like the reader to lose sight of the fact that there is a parallel between the situation that Melville described and the one that prevails now: human affection is regularly downgraded in the name of authority, and love is suppressed by power. The male couple, whether called homosexual or gay, remains a potentially subversive force against a society of male heterosexual domination that is committed to extend political and "scientific" control over all that it encounters. As Janet Todd has written of friendship between women, such same-sex friendship allows for "cooperation as well as conflict" and frees the woman from the need to construct "the feminine image she must create for a man."[10] For men, for whom the acquisition of a wife represents the highest conquest and who are trained to compete rather than to cooperate, the effect may be even greater. A man entering into a homosexual relationship abdicates, in part, his role in the economy of power; no longer controlling women, he must therefore "become" a woman. The fear he arouses comes from his demonstration of the arbitrariness of the connections between power and gender.

If, then, it is clear why I use the term "homosexual" and what I mean by it, there may still be some doubt about the appropriateness of the term as applied to Melville. We know that Melville was married and had four children; should this make us hesitate to use the term? In part any hesitation may reflect our twentieth-century model of exclusive sexualities. However, I should stress that my approach is in no way biographical and that what Melville actually "did" is of absolutely no literary significance. My analysis is at once textual and contextual: I want to situate what Melville wrote in the world he wrote of. But the only Melville I am concerned with is Melville the author of these works, to whom we have access through the works themselves. Recent biographical criticism of Melville, notably the biography by Edwin Haviland Miller, is so offensive as to make almost anyone doubt the method.[11] Miller assumes that all the works are but coded transcriptions of the life and that the life corresponds to a series of crises, all of which have already been described in the psychoanalytic literature. Rarely has criticism shown such contempt for its subject. Melville's works reveal, according to Miller, "an adolescent dream," "homoerotic arrestment," "an infantile whine," and so on. It is my own view that Melville's fundamental orientation was homosexual but that he found no way of realizing that desire *on land.* Only in the world of the ship could he experience the free expression of affection among men, and only in the "primitive" cultures of the South Seas could he see a society that gave an honorable place to male friendship. The encounter with Hawthorne, and his enthusiastic response to the older writer, indicate the one occasion when he may have felt it possible that his feelings might be satisfied within his world as a writer and an American. His feelings for Hawthorne, if we take the word of *Clarel* and its re-creation of the yearned-for seduction of Hawthorne/Vine by Melville/Clarel as well as the narrator's realization of Vine's inevitable rejection, possibly brought Melville to a clearer realization of the nature of his own sexuality and indeed to the greater sexual frankness of *Moby-Dick*. That novel, which all will agree is Melville's masterpiece, is an expression at once of enormous hope and enormous despair. Its very special qualities almost certainly owe a great deal to the seminal experience of Hawthorne. But here we deal with speculation, since we can never be absolutely certain of the reasons why a work takes the particular shape it does. It remains true, nonetheless, that Melville's later works seem haunted by the recollection of Hawthorne, just as Hawthorne's works seem repeatedly to justify a refusal of love for another man.

All of Melville's work is imbued with sexual awareness, although his sense of the demands for propriety on the part of his readers may well have led him to couch many of his references in guarded terms. There are phallic idols, from the *tiki* of *Typee* to Queequeg's Yojo; there are phallic jokes, most obviously in *Moby-Dick*, with its Sternean references to the unicorn presented to Queen Elizabeth and the lad for an archbishoprick; and the heroes themselves are imbued with phallic power, from Jack Chase in his disguise as Percy Main-Mast to Billy Budd, who recalls the worship of Baal. It is this element that requires that a discussion of male friendship in Melville's work go beyond the concept of romantic friendship. Certainly that concept, as seen, say, in Marryat's *Mr. Midshipman Easy* (1836), provided a basis from which to build as well as a safe context to which Melville's readers might have recourse if too troubled by the frank treatment of his novels. But two factors clearly distinguish the treatment of male friendship in Melville from that in earlier writers: the blatant association of friendship with sexuality in Melville and the assumption for male friendship of a subversive role with regard to the social order. In certain works in the friendship tradition, friendship is all heartiness and good fellowship without being sexual in the least, and far from being subversive, is seen as an integral part of social order. Given the differences between such works and his own, it is absurd to imagine that Melville was unaware of the sexual potential in male friendship; indeed his first novel includes a reference to Buggerry Island, later deleted (his willingness to delete some of the more obvious sexual references is an indication of his conscious use of them). The masculinity of his heroic figures is part of what endears them to him. This is so in part for simple erotic reasons; but it plays a larger role as well. Melville's work may be seen as a consistent appeal against the "feminization" or domestication of American culture.[12] His insistence on the presence of the phallus was a way of arguing for a reinvigoration of that society; male homosexuality is therefore used as a means of rejecting effeminacy. It should be noted as well that the emphasis on the phallus of which I speak is directed toward the kind of celebration of its erotic potential that is characteristic of matriarchal cultures. Other phallic figures—notably the harpoons and lances—also appear in Melville, but they are used in a very different way, as an element of male power.

Melville lacked a social context in which to locate homosexuality—either his own or that of his characters. The only place he had encountered a socially recognized homosexuality was in the South Seas, in the institution of the *tayo*. On shipboard he was aware of the way the system of "chums" allowed for the expression of affection between men and he was also aware of homosexual practices; but he correctly made no necessary connection between the two. The lack of a social context helps to explain the somewhat dreamlike treatment that he gives to his erotic male figures. In addition the antisocial nature of the homosexual relationship itself meant that there could be no way of situating that relationship within the larger society as it was then organized. And it was of course precisely to that antisocial nature that Melville appealed; his male couples are an essential part of the structure of his works as a way of institutionalizing the democratic instinct to union among equals and to the eventual fulfillment of that union in the overthrow of authority. The hierarchical order of the ship is endangered by the democratic order of the male couple, just as the heterosexual organization of society in the name of increased productivity is threatened by a homosexuality that promises to heal the divorce between work and play, production and pleasure.

Nineteenth-century writers on sex gave a specifically economic interpretation to male sexuality. To spend meant "to reach orgasm." As the middle classes were instructed in the virtues of thrift, so they were instructed in the thrifty use of sperm, it being assumed that each man possessed only a limited amount of sperm. Anything that might lead to the waste, or uneconomic use, of that sperm was to be discouraged. Hence "reverie was commonly held to lead to masturbation, the uneconomical expenditure of male creative power."[13] As reverie is thought unapplied to action, so masturbation is sperm unapplied to procreation, or capital uninvested. It is wise to bear these concepts in mind when approaching Melville's treatment of reverie. Far more than a modern reader may imagine, Melville's sexual politics oppose the dominant ideas of his time and display a deliberate and continued attempt to undermine the cult of earnest productivity. The role of all sexuality in Melville is subversive, and homosexuality, because of its antisocial nature and its uneconomic nature, is even more subversive. How then can it be allowed to flourish aboard a whaling ship, agent of what Newton Arvin has called "one of the great exploitative, wasteful, predatory industries of the nineteenth century"?[14]

The Quest for a Golden Island

Facts and Quests

What sort of books did Herman Melville write? The answer to that question has varied a great deal, from his own time to the present. In the nineteenth century Melville's works, particularly *Typee* and *Omoo*, were regarded as essentially factual accounts of real journeys. *Typee* remained in print precisely because of its presumed value as an accurate account of observations made on a real journey. It was cited in professional studies of ethnology and comparative religion, by authorities as eminent as Sir James Frazer and J. J. Bachofen.[1] With the revival of interest in Melville in the early twentieth century, it became possible to view *Typee* as a work of fiction, an apprentice work perhaps, but one nonetheless that bore certain relationships to Melville's by then more celebrated works, such as *Moby-Dick*, which were clearly viewed as fiction and not as fact. The monumental work of Charles Anderson, *Melville in the South Seas*, was able to show that Melville deliberately altered many of the facts of his own experience precisely because readers expected a claim to be made for the work as fiction.[2] *Typee*'s inaccuracies thus confirmed its nature as a work of art.

But one can perhaps go too far in the direction of proclaiming Melville's art, so far that one loses sight of its dense factuality, or at least its fiction of dense factuality. Because *Moby-Dick* is a work so obviously consistent with modern tastes—it has immediate appeal to the generation that read James Joyce's *Ulysses*, another sprawling, factual, mythic, dramatic epic of the search for reunion with the Parent—it is tempting to talk about all of Melville's work as if it were equally an experiment in narrative technique and point of view. While Melville does often experiment, drawing for instance on the techniques of Laurence Sterne, his works remain primarily Victorian in their seriousness of purpose and their moral directness. They are Victorian also in their bulk and in their unself-conscious pleasure in speaking. They are, quite frankly, garrulous and essayistic. What may seem to us self-conscious play of narrative level may be mere pauses to address the reader. Melville's forte, after all, was never plot (*Moby-Dick* is perhaps an exception to this rule). It is important, then, to stress Melville's employment of fact, and the appearance of fact, in order to understand the kind of tradition in which he worked. Among other things, Melville's early works should be thought of as belonging to the tradition of the travel narrative.[3] The period of mass travel in the nineteenth century, accompanying colonial expansion, brought increased interest on the part of readers to find out about the rest of the world. Many travel books also had religious, or quasi-religious themes, because they involved visits to holy places. The genre was extremely popular in the nineteenth century, probably because enough people traveled to make the thought of visiting such places not totally impossible, while not yet so many people traveled as to make the travel narrative unnecessary (it would be replaced in our time by the guide to hotels and restaurants, just as the Victorian emphasis of the Baedeker's on monuments that one must visit is replaced by places one must eat at). Within a few years of the publication of *Typee* (1846) Bayard Taylor undertook his journey to Egypt and the Holy Land, beginning the series of adventures that made him one of America's most celebrated authors, and George William Curtis published his *Nile Notes of a Howadji*, the first of his chronicles of his journeys to exotic places (both authors were part of Melville's New York literary circle).

Travel books should also be thought of as a possible Victorian form of genteel pornography. Under the guise of scientific reporting, the narrative of travel to exotic places allowed the writer to accomplish two things: to introduce an open sensuality that would otherwise be unthinkable in respectable literature (this role of the travel narrative was taken on in the twentieth century by *National Geographic* magazine, whose claim to reportorial truth allowed for the portrayal of nudity at a time when it would have been strictly forbidden in any other form), and to allow for a critique of dominant mores, whether Western colonialism or Protestant evangelism, by implied contrast. Indeed, one can say that much of nineteenth-century travel writing was implicitly subversive, in that it suggested some doubt about the superiority of Western, white cultures. Both of these functions were more than adequately performed by *Typee*: no American novel of the 1840s that was set in America seems likely to have been able to present so many naked bodies, so much open sex, so many phallic jokes and innuendoes; and only the claim of authenticity permitted Melville to demonstrate the hypocrisies of the Christian missions and the arrogance of the colonizing impulse.

A more specific need could also be served by the travel narrative, one that it has again continued to serve: the form permitted the exploration of alternate sexuality. For nineteenth-century homosexuals, in search of both a justification for themselves and a possible realization of their desires, the journey to an exotic landscape offered the possibility of locating a place where there might be others like them, a place where friendship might play its legitimate part in social life. As Newton Arvin put it in discreet terms, the "cult of physical beauty" that was associated with the Marquesas "implied inevitably a Greeklike cult of physical love also."[4] If Melville did not go to the South Seas in search of a homosexual paradise, his memory of his stay there included a nostalgic appreciation of a society in which deep friendship played an honorable part. The institutionalization of male friendship in Polynesia was known to Melville before his publication of *Typee*. In 1840 Richard Henry Dana included in *Two Years Before the Mast* an account of the institution he called *aikane* and Melville called *tayo*: the "one particular friend" whom one is "bound to do everything for," with whom one has "a sort of contract—an alliance offensive and defensive," and for whom one "will often make the greatest sacrifices."[5] This concept of a friendship contract remained important for Melville and obviously underlay his treatment of the Ishmael/Queequeg relationship in *Moby-Dick*. Melville was able to transform an idea presented largely in the context of social reporting into an idea that could serve as a basis for human action in any society. In *Typee* he remained fairly close to the terms outlined by Dana, although his treatment of male friendship goes beyond the specific institution of *tayo*. The narrator's *tayo*, Kory-Kory, is seen, with Western eyes, as a rather grotesquely tattooed figure, obviously anticipating Ishmael's initial response to Queequeg. But, although Tom recognizes the value of Kory-Kory's devotion, he is not able to move beyond his racial preconceptions; thus the element of sexual attractiveness is located not in Kory-Kory but rather in that other friend, Marnoo. By the time of *Moby-Dick* this split no longer occurs, in large part because the episode does not serve to illustrate Polynesian custom but rather the need for friendship as a means of survival in a hostile world. Melville almost certainly also knew about the conventions of friendship among North American Indians, and this connection between Polynesian and Indian customs was yet another element in the association between the two cultures that functioned so prominently in Melville's work. Melville was able to use the journey as a way of exploring the part that male friendship might play in the life of a man, if only he could be transported from the world of his own Western culture. Many of the tensions of *Typee* come from Melville's attempt to explore this theme and his inability to reach a full resolution of it.

In *Omoo* the subject is treated again, but with greater distance and a more "scientific" approach. Melville is closer to Dana and to the ethnographer's explanation of a strange custom. Still Melville dignifies the practice of special friendships by comparison—"In the annals of the island are examples of extravagant friendships, unsurpassed by the story of Damon and Pythias: in truth, much more wonderful" (p. 152). The narrator's *tayo*, Poky, is not grotesque, but "a handsome youth," and the narrator's departure leaves him standing alone, a figure of loss and sorrow at least equal to that of Fayaway. However, the later *tayo* shows that the practice may become corrupt, especially under the influence of the colonizers. All begins well with Kooloo, who is "a comely youth, quite a buck in his way" (p. 157). Despite Kooloo's claims for the extent of his love, he turns out to be faithless: "he had fallen in love at first sight with a smart sailor, who had just stepped ashore quite flush from a lucky whaling-cruise" (p. 158). There are gold diggers even in the islands of Paradise. *Omoo* makes no mythic use of this material, but then the entire work remains largely at the level of journal, never undergoing the artistic transformation attempted in *Typee*. Melville's great attention to the *tayo*, even here, indicates the fascination he felt for the subject, and his attempt to work it into his larger scheme of the search for happiness. In Melville's adaptation of the travel narrative, and despite his ability to transform it into a fictional form, the genre's implicit subversiveness becomes explicit. Melville never abandons his thick surface of facts because he needs them as a basis for his social criticism. While he may be creating a novel about the evils of colonialism and proselytism, he does so by demonstrating the very real evils of a recognizable colonial system or a recognizable system of Christian missions. Indeed the angry response of many readers indicated that Melville had indeed struck at something actual. And the reader of *Mardi* may occasionally wish, amidst the allegorizing, for some rock of fact on which to rest. But, at the same time, the danger inherent in Melville's preferred method is that it will be taken too narrowly. To some extent that has been the fate of these early books. Since the problems they describe are no longer topical, Melville's social and cultural perspectives may seem to be of little import. I believe that it is important to attempt to return to these books and recapture some of their sense of moral indignation. Melville is, after all, above all a moral writer, although not a conventional Christian— his sense of indignation often rises out of the sense of a Christian ideal betrayed by its very exponents. How can I be expected to believe, Melville seems to ask, in a system that seems to exist only in word and never in practice?

To read these works as mere topical critiques of specific flaws is to err as much in one way as to read them as abstract studies in literary method is in another. The works are topical; but they use their topical references as a way of building up an indictment of an entire social system based upon the superiority of one cultural group and the presumption that the "advanced" have a right to impose their way of life on the "primitive." Melville thus initiates the construction of a critique as radical as any that was to issue from his society, a critique that begins to connect the power of nationality, religion, culture, race, and gender. While Melville does not go quite so far as some of his readers have suggested, and is not a full-fledged primitivist, he is nonetheless quite unambiguous in his condemnation of the dominant culture of his time and radical in his suggestion that the cultures of the South Seas are worthy of investigation and respect.

If *Typee*, like *Omoo*, *White-Jacket*, and even *Moby-Dick* in part, is a novel drenched in facts, does this mean that it cannot also be seen in other, more literary ways? The answer, I think, is that the facts of these works do not in any way argue against their literary or mythic structures. The point is not to choose between an understanding of Melville's didactic purposes and an understanding of his literary purposes; the point is to discover how the two cohere. The fundamental literary structure of the travel narratives is, as I have termed it, the quest for a Golden Island. Because they are quests, the journey motif is an important one; and because it is for a Golden Island, that quest must in some sense be toward the past (the racial past of Typee corresponds to the lost youth/past of the hero as phylogeny corresponds to ontogeny). But the individual search for the Golden Island is hampered by a number of factors. The first of these is the interdiction on such exploration of forbidden territory. The Captain has warned his crew, like a father his children, not to stray beyond the line that divides civilization from savagery; the real fear here is not of course that the sailors will be killed but that they will become savages themselves, for that is the real threat to society, subversion from within. In *Typee* the individual desire to explore the valley of the Typees, in some sense to roam free in the preconscious, is in direct conflict with the social restrictions embodied in the Captain's authority. The second factor inhibiting the search for the Golden Island is the very fact that it is so clearly *other*, that the hero must inevitably remain the outsider, indeed in many ways the anthropologist. Tom can no more become a Typee, although he is adopted by the Typees, than we can recapture our own childhood, or undo the past. Tom's departure from Typee amounts to a recognition of the inevitable chasm between his experience elsewhere and his dreamlike existence in the happy valley.

If the Captain represents the authority of society that works against total abandonment of cultural identity, the Dark Stranger represents the erotic appeal of the unknown and the desire to escape beyond convention. In *Typee* the roles of these two figures seem at first glance less important than the anthropological data, but in fact they are inherently related. The Captain represents a particular kind of authority—a patriarchal authority that is specifically absent in Typee. That absence, Melville suggests, may have a great deal to do with the social harmony that exists there. The hero's attraction to the Dark Stranger(s) is a concrete way of expressing the role of the erotic as a subversive force to undermine that patriarchal authority. None of the alliances thus established is permanent enough to offer any real alternative to the Captain and so Tommo becomes Tom again and returns to the ship, abandoning his new friends. Many of these patterns are ones we shall see repeated: particularly the hero's abandonment of his friend, a clear indication of an ambivalence, either within Melville's sense of himself or in his evaluation of his hero's behavior (as in *Redburn*). Although escape to the Golden Island is only temporary, it does afford a first encounter with the Dark Stranger, marked with the sign of Life.

The structure of this pattern is largely Melville's own, but it also shows some indebtedness to the conventions of the captivity narrative. Like the earlier Puritan/frontier genre, Melville's travel books display a deep cultural ambivalence.[6] For the American Puritans who felt themselves physically threatened by the wilderness as well as spiritually threatened by its devilish inhabitants (the Indians), the captivity narrative expressed the fear not only of physical captivity, but, far more threatening, of the loss of identity. At the same time the Indian captive very often became a part of the tribe with which he (or more often she) lived—adopted as an honorary member or even wed to a chief's son or daughter. Many captives became Indians outright, and even those who returned often retained Indian habits and customs. Thus the rescue or escape, the ostensible goal of all captivity narratives, was frequently greeted with at least a degree of ambivalence; regaining one identity meant losing another. In *Typee* Melville made good use of the expectations of the form. Tom is adopted by the chief, Mehevi, and indeed given a new name, Tommo, signaling his change of identity. He is given a companion, or *tayo*, whose role is to serve as his bosom friend, as well as a "bride," Fayaway. These links to the Typees mean that his escape at the end is a betrayal of their friendship and trust and even, in some sense, of his own new self.[7] By shifting the site of the captivity narrative from the American frontier to the South Seas, Melville suggests how the continuing myth of the frontier functions in American culture, how it continues to operate simultaneously as an attraction and as a threat. At the same time this transposition in space makes the symbolic structure of the light/dark, civilized/primitive encounter even clearer. The fear is of "going native," of accepting the values of the "other"; and the intensity of the fear with which this idea is received reveals the precariousness of American cultural identity. The danger of going to Typee is that one may never want to come back; surely a society that feels this danger so intensely must doubt the validity of its own sense of self.

The relationship between Melville's narrative and the captivity narrative also draws attention to the way in which Melville was able to assimilate the experience of the American Indian into the experience of the South Sea Islander. This assimilation is important, since it lays the basis for the connections made in *Moby-Dick*, where Queequeg is at once Indian and South Sea Islander, and since it suggests the ways in which fact and myth coincide in Melville. For, as I have observed, the "facts" of life in the South Seas are given great attention in *Typee*: we get a kind of anthropologist's report on social customs, as well as a detailed description of setting, and even a map. These facts enable Melville to found his critique of colonial/missionary society in concrete observation; at the same time the mythic structures, suggested by Melville's links to the conventions of the Indian captivity narrative, suggest the wider meanings of the novel. For an American, the first, and most important, experience of cultural aggression and racial decimation remains the encounter of the whites with the Indians, an encounter that results in the elimination of almost all Indian culture as well as of most Indians: this stark fact, and its moral burden, must underlie any serious treatment of the theme of self and world, as we can see hinted at in *The Scarlet Letter* or *The House of the Seven Gables* and made explicit in Hart Crane's *The Bridge* or the novels of William Faulkner. Since American society's "progress" across the continent is based on aggression, theft, and murder, and since it can very accurately be depicted as the rape of the land and its (her) inhabitants, it is difficult for Melville to comprehend the extent of Western horror at the purported barbarism of nonwhite cultures. The appeal of Typee is precisely that of a nonaggressive, communal society in which affection plays a large part. That the novel ends in a return to the world of the Captain, to the world of "civilized" order, indicates the efficacy of the "escape from captivity" motif, both as narrative excitement and as cultural stability, but it cannot prevent the work from creating its overall effect of longing. The culture that is lost is that of the Typees; it is back on board ship that one is truly in captivity.

Typee: The Structure of the Encounters

The novel begins with two comic encounters that establish the theme of mutual incomprehension. In the one, the missionary's wife is the subject of great interest on the part of all the islanders until they attempt to look beneath her voluminous petticoats. She interprets their curiosity as a violation of her person and retreats to civilization; meanwhile the islanders are disappointed by their discovery of an ordinary woman. While Melville does not specify what they expected to find, it is possible that they expected her to be a man beneath all those layers of concealment. Whether they expected a sacred *berdache* or a divine androgyne, it is clear that they are distressed to find a mere mortal woman. The second of the encounters involves the queen, who is fascinated by a sailor's tattooing and decides to show him her own—on her ass! She does not recognize that the ass is a "taboo" part of the anatomy for the whites and so inadvertently transgresses a rule of social behavior. In each case people behave according to their own rules and are unaware how their actions will be perceived in a different social context. In part, therefore, Melville begins his novel by episodes that illustrate cultural relativism. However, they also establish a fundamental part of his social critique of Western culture: in both cases the Westerners see a sexual gesture where none is intended. In both cases they prefer concealment to display, taking display as a sign of sexual freedom. The episodes, in their comic way, make it clear that the sexual obsessions lie in the minds of the Westerners and not in the gestures of the islanders.

Throughout the novel Melville works toward the reversal of expectations. Where his audience may expect a sense of danger in the arrival on a primitive island, instead he provides a scene of generalized pleasure as the women swim out to the boat, displaying "wild grace and spirit" (p. 15). Melville pauses in his narrative to comment on the fate of those who unwittingly rejoice in the arrival of the visitors, and he speaks here in the editorial voice that so often steps forward to comment on the events and underscore their meaning:

When the inhabitants of some sequestered island first descry the "big canoe" of the European rolling through the blue waters towards their shores, they rush down to the beach in crowds, and with open arms stand ready to embrace the strangers. Fatal embrace! They fold to their bosoms the vipers whose sting is destined to poison all their joys; and the instinctive feeling of love within their breasts is soon converted into the bitterest hate.

Two cultures meet here, under the symbols of the embrace and the viper, figures of love and betrayal. The horror of the Europeans' behavior is magnified by these images of an innocence abused and betrayed. And whatever hatred may finally be shown by the islanders is not laid to native malice but rather to the anger at this betrayal by those whom they have loved. It cannot pass notice here that this symbolic figure of the meeting of these two cultures recapitulates in miniature form the encounter of European and Indian that lies at the base of American history. Melville's use indeed of the term "European" here strengthens this allusion to a prefiguration of this episode. If Americans are hated by the Indians of their land, the passage suggests, they have only their own behavior to blame.

The introductory chapters of *Typee* thus establish the social context for the inner story of the escape (or captivity) of Tom and Toby. They are important not only as a way of giving credibility but as a way of providing an interpretive structure for the story of journey, quest, and magical realm. The society from which Tom and Toby come is already identified as one of confused sexuality, moral self-righteousness, and ingratitude. Thus their departure from the ship and the "unmitigated tyranny" (p. 21) of the Captain is no mere adventure or personal whim; it is founded in a political and social reality. If the Captain represents the "tyranny" of Western political authority, the alternative to that authority is quickly established in terms of comradeship. Toby is presented as the first of the Dark Strangers, even though he is present on the ship, and it is he who is able to function as a guide for the passage from the world of the ship to that of the island. The description of Toby makes his symbolic role clear: "His naturally dark complexion had been deepened by exposure to the tropical sun, and a mass of jetty locks clustered about his temples, and threw a darker shade into his large black eyes" (p. 32). The repeated images of darkness show that Toby is already in some sense an islander. Tom's decision to flee the ship with Toby is his first commitment to the exploration of values opposed to those of Western authority. That Toby is also physically attractive suggests the way in which the erotic operates as a counterforce to the rule of conventional authority: his "remarkably prepossessing exterior" is of course the outward manifestation of an inner virtue, a kind of natural nobility that is present in all of Melville's Dark Strangers.

Melville's jocular reference to "Buggerry Island" makes it clear that he was aware of homosexual practices on shipboard (there are references to this in *White-Jacket*, as well). But it is also clear that he does not connect the reference to practices with the desire that the novel expresses for an idealized homosexuality or male friendship. Although, in the absence of the term "homosexuality," buggery and sodomy were the only terms possible to describe such activity, it seems that Melville distinguished between homosexual practices such as might occur on shipboard, frequently involving force and arising more out of necessity than out of affection, and a passionate love of men that he repeatedly described as an ideal and sought a place for. *Typee* suggests that some form of that affection might be possible, even on shipboard, although a pursuit of its fulfillment would seem to lead inevitably to escape from the ship and to the exploration of the island with a dark companion.

Tom thinks of escaping alone, but then considers the need for a friend—a "partner of my adventure," "some comrade with me," "what solace would a companion be!" When Tom and Toby have agreed to undertake an escape together, "we ratified our engagement with an affectionate wedding of palms" (p. 33). The repeated use of a similar metaphor in that phrase—"engagement" and "wedding"—anticipates Melville's use of the marriage metaphor to join Ishmael and Queequeg in *Moby-Dick*. There are other links to the later novel, which help to show that this early novel, although lacking much of the verbal brilliance of the later work, is not totally different in theme. The double (or triple) structure of Dark Strangers in *Typee* is replaced, of course, by the single figure of Queequeg, but the union of Tom and Toby is the first suggestion of a joining together of opposites that plays a large symbolic role in all Melville's novels. And, in anticipation of the opening of *Moby-Dick*, we first see Toby "leaning over the bulwarks, apparently plunged in a profound reverie" (p. 31). As a water gazer, Toby suggests, in skeletal form, the significance of the Narcissus figure that will be elaborated into one of the symbolic centers of *Moby-Dick*. Here the image serves to strengthen our sense of Toby as a mirror self, a darker version of the Hero. By following Toby, then, Tom is enabled to discover something about himself.

Toby's reverie appears to have carried greater connotations for nineteenth-century readers than it may for us. As G. J. Barker-Benfield puts it, commenting on Ik Marvel's *Reveries of a Bachelor* (1850), "Reverie was commonly held to lead to masturbation, the uneconomical expenditure of male creative power."[8] Whether or not Melville expected his readers to make this specific association (and the possibility is not remote, as will be seen in my discussion of Toby's role as a "rover"), the figure of the handsome, dark, brooding figure staring at the sea suggests a strong sensuality that is sharply contrasted to the world of work under the control of the Captain. Toby is the first manifestation of the link between the erotic and the subversive, and it is because of that link that he is able to lead the way toward the Golden Island.

The beginning of *Typee* bears a striking resemblance to Poe's *Narrative of Arthur Gordon Pym*—a vision of mixed delight and horror and a response to that vision by an "irresistible curiosity" (p. 5). (*Pym*, too, brings the narrator into a central relationship with a Dark Stranger, of distinctly phallic name, Dirk Peters, by means of an intermediate guide.) The mixture of delight and horror that is the response to Typee is presented as a realistic detail, but it serves equally well as a depiction of a psychic state. For the narrator, Tom, is pulled toward the images of natural beauty, lushness, and pleasure. But these cannot be attained without the commission of a crime—the abandonment of the ship. As a sailor on a whaling ship, Tom is not free; he is at the mercy of his captain. His captain, like the others in Melville's work, exercises a power of life and death over his crew and is subject to no constraints on his behavior. The tyranny of the captain, his cruelty, the inequities of social class that seem even more acute on board ship than on land, contribute to Tom's decision to leave the ship. And yet an element of terror is implicit, for the Captain warns of the fate of those who leave the ship behind. The rumor of the cannibalism of the islanders is a means of social control, as well as an externalization of the fear that must accompany such an important act of social transgression. The danger of being eaten by cannibals is the danger of losing one's body and soul—if, as seems almost certain, Melville knew *Pym*, he was familiar with the cannibalism there that marks a stage in the spiritual journey to the other, *white* side of the world. Knowing the terror, and yet almost attracted by it, the young men extend their journey to the second stage: for the journey on the ship to the South Seas is only a first, virtual frame narration; the second journey is the one that Tom and Toby take to the heart of otherness, the heart of the forbidden and appealing island.

In the virtual absence of the presentation of any world on shore, the ship takes the place of society. The ship is not a means of escaping society (as in adventure stories), but society itself. And that society is, we see, one of strict regimentation and authoritarianism. It is, in that sense, like a family, for, Melville frequently reminds us, the Captain is a father to his crew. This potential "paradise of bachelors" is spoiled by the presence of the Captain, representing the interdictions of society. The first act required, or desired, is an assertion of self and a gratification of desire, through the abandonment of authority. In order to gratify his desire, Tom must become a criminal. That this act does not *seem* criminal is irrelevant, as is the fact that there is no criminal intent. The rule of the Captain is absolute, from *Typee* to *Billy Budd*, and therefore natural good (as represented by Typee or by Billy) is always in conflict with social good (as represented by the Captain). Putting it another way, the gratification of desire, the search for pleasure, the Quest for the Golden Land, is always antisocial. The conflict is essential to Melville's work, for he seems to have recognized early the insight that would later be developed by Freud that personal desires must always be suppressed by society in order to provide the additional energy needed for work. The threat to society throughout Melville is the threat of play—play for its own sake. Play carries with it the notion of a self-sufficient or narcissistic eroticism, and thus it is not surprising that nineteenth-century moralists made a connection between reverie and masturbation. For it is certain that play threatens work precisely as sexuality threatens the economic structure; neither can be eliminated, but both need to be circumscribed and relegated to a restricted time of life (childhood or youth) or transformed into a new, socially useful form by making them productive rather than pleasurable in themselves. From *Typee* on, Melville recognizes that the world of play has become infinitely smaller (both historically and in individual lives) and that the "fathers" will do all they can to punish those who defect, who run away from responsibility. In *Typee* Melville has his hero make the choice for freedom and play, but he bears with him signs of his divided mind: his swollen leg, symbol of his wounded nature and also of his inability to function as "natural" man, and his constant fears that he will be eaten by the natives or that he will be tattooed. Both of these may be thought of as castration fears but are more usefully viewed as impediments to his integration into the Typee community, signs that although he has defected from the ship, he has not entirely defected from its values. The fear of being eaten, half-comic and half-horrific, seems to be largely a displacement of the fear of eating human flesh, that is, of partaking of some dark sacred meal. Tom escapes before he can commit this final transgression, the step that would appear to make him irrevocably a Typee.[9]

Tom's companion on these adventures, Toby, has no problem with his leg and is apparently far less guilt-ridden than the narrator. Although one of the sailors, he is spiritually closer to the natives. His dark skin, "deepened by exposure," indicates that his relationship with Tom is a prelude to the relationships between Tom and the natives of Typee as well as the first indication of Melville's fundamental structure of the relationship between two young men—generally a white, European "intellectual" and a more "natural" darker Oriental or Mediterranean. Whatever the facts about the real Toby's disappearance from Typee (some of them given in Melville's "Sequel"), it is clear that the symbolic role of Toby ends once the couple has reached the interior of the island. Toby is a guide and an intermediary. His darkness signals his affinities to the natural world of Typee, and his lack of origins marks him off as someone not fixed either in the world of the ship or that of the island. "He was one of that class of rovers you sometimes meet at sea, who never reveal their origin, never allude to home, and go rambling over the world" (p. 32). According to John Todd, minister in Pittsfield and important religious writer on sexuality (he was Melville's apparent object of satire in "The Lightning-Rod Man"), "a roving imagination led to reverie and habitual masturbation."[10] It seems quite likely that Melville's reference to Toby as a "rover" includes at least an association with a free sensuality. Anyone so clearly separated from the values of "home" is necessarily liberated from the associated concepts of domesticity, hence freed to the kind of unlimited masculinity that Victorian theorists saw manifested in masturbation. To "rove" was at the very least to be promiscuous and hence to be a threat to the domestic economy. The words of the well-known sea song "A-Roving" suggest that the association between "roving" and sexuality was well established:

> A-roving, a-roving
> Since roving's been my ruin,
> I'll go no more a-roving
> With you, fair maid.[11]

Toby is in any case a free spirit. It is precisely this freedom that the novel presents as its highest value. Tommo's escape, although partly motivated by fear, is also a sign of his refusal to be "typed," to become a Typee. He too must learn to rove. The title of Melville's subsequent volume, *Omoo*, indeed, means "rover" in Polynesian, according to Melville, and indicates the extent to which Tom "becomes" Toby—or at least the hero of *Omoo*, revolting against his inadequate and incompetent captain and lingering in the South Seas, takes on many of Toby's qualities. Still later, Pip will call Queequeg a "rover" (*Moby-Dick*, p. 397).

If Toby is important as a guide toward the discovery of the Golden Island, he is also important as a means for escape from the Captain. But this opposition is not only a personal one, just as the story of *Typee* should not be considered to be the story of Tom and Toby with a decorative backdrop of information about the colonization of the islands. Melville begins his novel with the encounter of two cultures, and that theme persists throughout the novel. It is the role of the Dark Strangers to help lead the Heroes of Melville's works away from the corrupt civilizations they have inhabited. By bringing Tom to Typee, the Dark Stranger allows the Hero to experience for himself a different culture and to enjoy that open embrace that first greeted the ship as it entered the harbor. Escape from the Captain means not only release into a world where play is valued but also release from a world of aggression and death. For, as the narrator puts it, "The fiend-like skill we display in the invention of all manner of death-dealing engines, the vindictiveness with which we carry on our wars, and the misery and desolation that follow in their train, are enough of themselves to distinguish the white civilized man as the most ferocious animal on the face of the earth" (p. 125). Although the occasion for this exclamation may be Melville's study of the effects of colonization, it is clear that his target is a larger one; it is all the crimes committed in the name of civilization by the "white civilized man" whose belief in his superior race, culture, and gender has allowed him to commit unspeakable crimes against humanity. Again and again one must remind oneself that Melville is concerned in his treatment of the South Seas with a case of virtual cultural genocide; he sees this deathblow not as an exception or a rare excess of power, but as a characteristic act of a culture based on certain values. Even in the incomplete terms of *Typee*, it is clear that Melville's purpose is to awaken the conscience of his readers to the horrors of their own society and to begin the search for an alternative.

With the help of Toby, Tom can flee the ship and begin the journey to the interior of the island. The extraordinary difficulties of this journey again remind us of *Pym* and illustrate the novel's maintenance of a romance structure of myth alongside its dense factuality. It has been pointed out that Melville's real-life journey was a relatively simple one, but the myth required an elaborate, painstaking journey. For the Golden Land must be secret, difficult of access, and enclosed. The journey there must be perilous, so that those who journey are worthy of their rare reward. Part of the evocative power of the journey in *Typee* comes from the particular forms it takes. Melville's preferred location for the Golden Land is a version of what W. H. Auden has called the "garden-island." In Auden's view, this image joins the qualities of the garden, its solitude, enclosure, and innocence, to the qualities of the island, its safety and its exemption from ordinary law. It is characteristic of the garden-island that "there is no conflict between natural desire and moral duty."[12] By introducing Tom/

Tommo into the island paradise, Melville creates a conflict for his protagonist. Tommo can recognize the identity of natural desire with life on
Typee, but Tom cannot escape the recollection of moral duty, or what he
takes to be moral duty. For Tom/Tommo moral duty and natural desire
seem irreconcilable, and so life with the Typees is ultimately impossible.

Although Tom is unable to remain there, Melville repeatedly treats
Typee in terms of its superiority to "civilized" society. In every possible
way he establishes the contrast between the two worlds, always to the
advantage of Typee and to the disadvantage of civilization. The images are
those traditionally associated with the Golden Land—lush vegetation,
calm, peace, tranquility. Typee is "like the enchanted garden in the fairy
tale." It is like "the gardens of Paradise" (p. 49). The prelapsarian implications are repeated: "The penalty of the Fall presses very lightly upon the
valley of Typee" (p. 195). And Melville goes on to identify specifically its
unfallen nature: "I scarcely saw any piece of work performed there" (p.
195). The native women have "unconcealed natural graces" compared to
the "stiffness, formality, and affectation" of "coronation beauties, at West-
minster Abbey" (p. 161). Beauty and grace are not the only points of
Typee's superiority; its inhabitants also demonstrate superior virtue, a trait
they share with other "barbarous people," Melville asserts. "The hospitality of the wild Arab, the courage of the North American Indian, and the
faithful friendships of some of the Polynesian nations, far surpass any
thing of a similar kind among the polished communities of Europe" (pp.
202–3). Because it is a function of his own attitude to himself and his
culture, Tommo's perception of Typee is subject to radical shifts. He believes he has entered Paradise, then he feels he has fallen among cannibals;
his leg swells, then his leg heals; he comes to understand something of
Typee life, and then suddenly he fears for his survival (the survival of his
identity much more than that of his life). This vacillation is between two
extremes, neither of which can be accurate. Each of the tribes sees the
other as the enemy and defines evil in terms of otherness. Are we with the
good tribe or the evil tribe? Melville's point of course is that no tribe (read
nation) is ever good or evil; each has its peculiar customs that may seem
evil to those who do not understand them. The novel moves toward a
recognition of the complexity of experience, a complexity that precludes
simple categorization. Melville plays on the problem of naming in his
reference to the tribal name:

> Their very name is a frightful one; for the word "Typee" in the
> Marquesan dialect signifies a lover of human flesh. It is rather
> singular that the title should have been bestowed upon them

exclusively, inasmuch as the natives of all this group are irre-
claimable cannibals. The name may, perhaps, have been given to
denote the particular ferocity of this clan, and to convey a special
stigma along with it. [pp. 22–23]

This explanation of the name is one of Melville's inventions. Its fictiveness
serves to stress its importance in Melville's symbolic structure. The name
creates the fear; it is the category that determines our perceptions. The
other tribes condemn the Typees by labeling them; newcomers cannot
help meeting them with fear and hostility. The fear of cannibalism recurs
in *Moby-Dick*, where it is treated with unambiguous comedy; there too
Ishmael's response to Queequeg as a headhunter is based upon a label that
precedes experience. In *Moby-Dick* Melville would move toward an analysis of the function of language in the establishment of systems of authority; here he begins his exploration by simply urging that true perception requires as much as possible an experience not contaminated by the
preconceptions imposed by language.

There is a further ambiguity about this reference. As Paul Witherington
has pointed out in a brief but fascinating comment, Melville seems to
suggest a double meaning here: it is, he says, "an ambiguity that suggests
either cannibalism or sensuality and, more important, the cannibalism *of*
sensuality, a paradox crucial to the novel."[13] The Typees are, indeed, lovers
of flesh, and their voluptuousness evokes as much fear as their reputed
cannibalism. To see the Typees correctly, one must forget one's preconceptions, which means, abandon all labels (just as *Moby-Dick* cannot be
known by its etymology or library classification). By analogy, in order to
see homosexuality correctly one must forget preconceptions and categories of good and evil; homosexuality is both buggery and ideal friendship.
The Tom who flees at the end succumbs both to his sexual fears and to his
cultural prejudices.

Because of the great difference between what the narrator reports about
life on Typee and the hero's behavior, critics have often disagreed about
the novel's statement on issues involving the conflict between the "primitive" and the "civilized." The early critics of the Melville revival, such as
Charles Anderson, generally assumed that the work should be read as
what Anderson calls a "brief against civilization." In this view, *Typee* is part
of a Romantic tradition that makes use of a primitive culture as a way of
indicting civilization. Encouraged perhaps by the primitivist spirit of the
1920s, which sought an escape from the false "progress" of Western civilization, Anderson made the classic case for the novel as a defense of the
primitive: for him *Typee* is "a whole-hearted defense of the Noble Savage

and a eulogy of his happy life, his external beauty, and his inward purity of heart."[14] Hardly anyone would put the argument in quite such enthusiastic terms now, but it remains true that no statement about Typee or the Typees is critical of that society. It remains equally true that Melville used the moral superiority of the islands as a way of attacking the presumed superiority of his own society.

More recent critics, however, have frequently argued against the primitivist reading of *Typee*, although their evidence, aside from Tom's departure, is slight. Milton Stern, for instance, writes, "The cliché, the flip 'philosophy' about the undressed-savage-as-happier-man-than-beribboned-admiral is relatively unimportant. It is glib and traditional, and, as it appears here, cheap and shoddy."[15] Unfortunately, his comments do not say much more than that he does not like primitivism; he is not even able to deny its existence in the novel, merely its importance or value. It must be remembered that if primitivism seemed "traditional" in the 1950s when Stern was writing, it seemed much less so in the 1840s. The fact is that Melville's readers did not take his critique of Western society and of Christian missions lightly; their fury, and the need to excise many of these references from later editions of the book, indicate that Melville's pro-primitive position was still seen as dangerously marginal. What is more, it is never "glib" since it is always clearly located in the specific observation of both the islands' virtues and, more importantly, civilization's failures. Stern believes that the conclusion of the novel indicates that primitivism is "rejected" in *Typee*; this analysis is consistent with his view that Billy Budd is a narcissist, while Nelson and Vere display "selfless circumspection."[16] Edwin Miller, in his biography of Melville, concludes that a Rousseau-based primitivism is not actually present in Melville's works, for, "despite the attacks upon civilization and vague statements seeming to support Rousseau's romanticism, Melville did not take the French philosopher to heart: there was too much of the puritan and the Calvinist in his nature."[17] But the novels from *Typee* to *Moby-Dick* reveal that Melville consistently used primitive cultures as a way of criticizing a Calvinist culture (what he called "Presbyterian" in *Moby-Dick*). His statements in support of such a position, far from being "vague," are specific in their praise of natural beauty, grace, manners, the absence of violence, the absence of property-based values, and the dominance of brotherhood as fundamental concepts of human relations.

There is one clearly defined Noble Savage in *Typee*, who illustrates Melville's indebtedness to Rousseau and his appropriation of the idea of the Noble Savage for his own purposes. The Noble Savage is Marnoo, the stranger. He is, as the concept implies, a strange mixture of the savage with classical ideals of beauty. He has "matchless symmetry of form," he might have stood for the "statue of the Polynesian Apollo," he reminds Tom of "an antique bust" (p. 135). His striking beauty is tempered by a cheek "of a feminine softness," hinting at the androgyny that Melville associated with the realization of the ideal. Here, then, is Nature's nobleman, and Tom is immediately smitten, only to be sorely disappointed when Marnoo appears to pay him no attention: "Had the belle of the season, in the pride of her beauty and power, been cut in a place of public resort by some supercilious exquisite, she could not have felt greater indignation than I did at this unexpected slight" (p. 136). Marnoo is not quite as unreceptive as he at first seems. He tells the story of his life to Tom (like Toby, he has no family and no origins, he was an islander who was "carried to sea," he is another rover, and he is a man between two cultures, embodying the best of both). And he is eventually the means of Tom's escape.

The composite figure, Marnoo / Toby, represents Melville's ideal. Each of them is somewhere between civilization and savagery. Marnoo, for instance, has the Polynesian beauty (which the narrator identifies with Greek beauty), but he does not have the usual facial tattoos. He does have one very striking tattoo, though, a tree that is traced along his spine, suggesting to the narrator a "spreading vine tacked against a garden wall" (p. 136). Marnoo is thus identified as a life force, bearing the tree of life. He retains the original phallic power that is otherwise disappearing from the Islanders. Neither pure native nor pure civilized white, Marnoo (like his prototype Toby) points to a union of the best of both worlds, black and white, male and female, classical and romantic. His phallic potential is there as a positive force, neither destroyed as in the idols, nor grotesquely aggressive as in the adaptation of phallic energy to colonial conquest. In a fascinating passage, anticipating the black god of Queequeg, Melville discusses one of the ithyphallic idols. It is in the traditional shape, but "all its prominent points were bruised and battered, or entirely rotted away. The nose had taken its departure . . . " (p. 178). Allowing for the prudishness of his readers, Melville seems to be as clear as he can be: the idol or *tiki* has lost its phallus (Poe used the nose as an elaborate phallic joke in just the same way, we recall), just as the Typee society has lost its phallic potency. Melville then turns it all into a delightful joke, bemoaning "the wood-rot malady" as a sign of a "back-slidden generation . . . sunk in religious sloth, and requir[ing] a spiritual revival," in a wonderful parody of the language of American evangelism. Only those few rare souls, like Marnoo, who can transcend the traditional boundaries, are able to achieve the highest state in which such a revival of spiritual and erotic energy can truly take place. It is in the intermediate state, the union of civilization and savagery, rather than the victory of one or the other, that true beauty resides. Melville's vision here, as in *Moby-Dick*, is of a triumphant miscegenation in which the opposites of Western, and particularly American, history will be reconciled: in *Typee* that mystic marriage is presented in a single individual, and his relationship to the white hero/narrator is only implied. As the novels progress in time, Melville moves toward a more direct depiction of this miscegenation in terms of an actual male couple.

This theme reaches its fullest statement in the "marriage" of Ishmael and Queequeg. Queequeg is the logical conclusion of all the Dark Strangers and lovers throughout Melville's early works, and he bears with him his god, sign both of his savagery and his phallic potency (thus giving rise to all sorts of hilarious castration fears on the part of Ishmael, just as cannibalism and tattooing provide a delicious shudder in *Typee*). By his marriage to Ishmael, the South Seas are wedded to New England, primitive to Presbyterian, body to soul. But the assertion of the need for such a union runs through Melville's works. It is already present in Tommo's admiration for Marnoo and in Marnoo's part in Tommo's escape. From the patriarchal world of the ship, Tommo escapes to the matriarchal affections of Typee. But he is never free of the fear of retribution. What prevents the novel from fulfilling its dream of a union that begins the process of healing century-old wounds is what appears to be something like a Calvinist conscience on the part of Tom that makes him doubt the virtues of a society devoted to pleasure. That doubt, which seems to be deliberately attributed by Melville to his character and not merely transferred from his own consciousness, together with what seems to me Melville's inability to deal with the novel's inescapably homosexual implications, drives Tom back to the ship, abandoning the benign phallicism of a matriarchal society for the phallic aggression that comes to dominate *Moby-Dick*.

The recently discovered manuscript of parts of *Typee*[18] reveals how fully Melville devoted himself to praise of a benign phallic world in his early drafts, even though these were later revised in the probable interests of propriety. The famous scene in chapter 14 in which Kory-Kory jealously watches as the "nymphs" anoint Tommo's body originally included a reference to "transport," later changed to "delight" (and another to "delight" replaced by the euphemistic "kindness"). This same scene included Tommo's association of his own situation with that of Captain Macheath in *The Beggar's Opera* (Melville cites the final aria, "Thus I stand like the Turk / With his doxies around"), Sardanapalus, and the Sultan. The episode is a remarkable paean to a passive receptivity, a masturbation that is ostensibly performed by the women but is certainly presided over by the spirit of Kory-Kory. It is Melville's celebration of a polymorphous and undirected sexuality that is directly related to the social order of Typee. It is one of the sources of the "sperm-squeezing" episode in *Moby-Dick*. Immediately following the scene of the anointing Melville presents the scene called "Producing Light à la Typee," another remarkably erotic passage. David Ketterer has already called attention to the phallic imagery in this passage,[19] but an examination of the manuscripts reveals that the original language was even more open than the version eventually published. For instance, Melville originally wrote "attains his climax" where the text now reads "approaches the climax of his effort" (p. 111). Thus a second masturbation, in the manuscript clearly performed for the reader's "particular gratification," follows the first scene of erotic arousal. In both cases Melville draws our attention to a self-sufficient and socially integrated sexuality that stands in sharp contrast to the Western world of shame. As Melville laughingly points out, these practices of phallic celebration would seem to be appropriately attended by a "college of vestals" were it not for "special difficulties"—presumably the lack of any virgins.

Unlike the later works, *Typee* does not indicate a Melville who was prepared to explore the meaning of male friendship in its deepest implications. He could joke about buggery, he could show ideal, handsome companions, but he could not bring the two together. It is a sign of the tentative nature of Melville's exploration of sexual issues here that a good deal of attention is given to Fayaway (the only other novel prior to *Pierre* with important women characters is the allegorical *Mardi*). This is not to say that Fayaway is a false character, merely that she is not drawn with the same passionate conviction as the male characters and that she does not fill a place in Melville's symbolic universe. Conventionally beautiful, she is "the very perfection of female grace and beauty" and every feature is "as perfectly formed as the heart or imagination of man could desire" (p. 85). Melville's heart is simply not in those generalized descriptions that create nothing more convincing for us than the traditional figure of romance. Still, it is important to note that Melville does give her an independence that marks her off from the heroines of more "civilized" countries. And his depiction of her sorrow at Tommo's departure does seem actually felt; there is perhaps a perception of the degree of deception involved in that romance and the inevitable need to leave such a lover behind. Are we sure that Tommo could have resisted a similar call from Marnoo? Melville, at the time of writing *Typee*, was apparently not prepared to depict the world of exclusive male friendship and sexuality that would characterize his later works. He sought to express in his first novel a work of released sexual pleasure, one in which the body could be celebrated and in which individuals could be free to explore their deeper natures. In this world, partly observed and partly imagined, Fayaway, the beautiful woman, could take her place alongside Kory-Kory, the faithful friend, and Marnoo, the handsome stranger.

The existence of such an autonomous figure as Fayaway may be one of the many indications that Melville gives in *Typee* that the society he depicts had been matriarchal at some not so distant time. The traces of matriarchal religion are evident, although power at the time of his narrative seems to reside in the men, and women are excluded from the sacred grove, and from the canoe. One of the novel's striking scenes has Tommo and Fayaway violate the taboo by sailing together, one of Melville's few deliberate violations of likely historical accuracy. The scene serves to emphasize Melville's use of the novel to explore a critique of social organization and sexual convention. Melville notices the existence of a system of polyandry, and he is perceptive enough to see its implications. He begins his discussion of marriage customs by noting that the unit is normally composed of two men and one woman. After a young couple has been formed, an older man comes along and carries them off to his house. "This disinterested and generous-hearted fellow," Melville remarks facetiously, "now weds the young couple—marrying damsel and love at the same time—and all three henceforth live together as harmoniously as so many turtles" (p. 191). The description of apparently bisexual men may be colored by Melville's own tastes, but he moves quickly to see the larger social implications, for this "plurality of husbands" "speaks volumes for the gentle disposition of the male population." Melville concludes on something of a comic note by suggesting the possibility of male harems, but concluding of American men, "we are scarcely amiable and forbearing enough to submit to it" (p. 191). Despite the joking tone, Melville's references make it clear that he recognizes the arbitrariness of male domination—and the mere suggestion of the opposite patterns of female domination, so feared by men, should be enough to display its foolishness and intolerable nature. Melville is radical enough to suggest that the aggressive behavior of men is related to the Western concept of marriage. The acquisition of a bride becomes the first step in the development of a system of private property and of the defense of that private property by force if necessary. On Typee, on the other hand, private ownership of anything other than personal articles does not seem to exist. Land is apparently held "in fee simple from Nature herself" (p. 202) until, of course, the colonists seize it. When men are not competing for the ownership of women, Melville suggests, they are free to develop friendships among themselves, friendships like those of Polynesia described in *Typee* and *Omoo*.

Melville's myth of the Golden Land is intricately tied up with his notion of male friendship. Toby was not, apparently, the mere random companion Melville tries to depict. Melville thought enough of the real Toby, Richard Tobias Greene, to keep a daguerreotype of him until his death, where it was found among his possessions.[20] Late in his life he wrote a very moving poem to Toby, now called (in an amusing erotic pun) Ned Bunn, in which he recalls their journey to "Marquesas and glenned isles that be / Authentic Edens in a pagan sea." He recognizes that their world has passed with time and that tourists now take the place of the earlier voyagers, but he still recalls with pleasure the Paradise they once knew:

> But we, in anchor-watches calm,
> The Indian Psyche's languor won,
> And, musing, breathed primeval balm
> From Edens ere yet overrun;
> Marvelling mild if mortal twice,
> Here and hereafter, touch a Paradise.

The sense of Paradise lost here is double, of course, for he has lost not only the Paradise that all men lose, the paradise that the Bible calls Eden, but also the paradise of male friendship that he knew with Ned/Toby. Many people have the sense that growing older involves a sense of loss, but when growth implies the abandonment of a potential for deep affection, as Melville felt in his own life, the sense of loss is particularly acute. The South Seas were for Melville at least three things, in ascending order of abstraction: the place I was with Ned, the place where male friendship is recognized and institutionalized, and the place where we all lived once, where there was plenty to eat, warmth and sunshine, happiness and harmony. These ideas are inseparable for an understanding of Melville's first novel. They are the elements that enable Melville to transform his material from social satire into a vision, if still somewhat fogged, of an alternate world that may come to replace the rule of Captains, colonial governors, and missionaries.

Fact or fiction? Defense of innocence or rejection of the primitive? Like Melville's later work, *Typee* evades easy definition. The "facts" of *Typee* provide a basis for Melville's critique of society and a justification for his violation of Victorian taboos. Its "fictions" enable Melville to make his own use of this material and to turn an apparent travel narrative into the symbolic exposition of a spiritual autobiography. Although Melville's narrator does not have the ability to deal fully with the sexuality of the tale he himself relates, he does make a giant step forward when he comes to recognize the impossibility of judging by appearances. There can be no answer to the good/evil dilemma of Typee, since the dilemma itself is false. There is only experience. By bearing in mind, however, that innocence stands, among other things, for homosexuality (although a homosexuality that is itself in some sense "innocent"), one can understand Melville's problem and the confusion of his critics. *Typee* is a work that proposes the superiority of a "savage" morality over a "civilized" one, but one that must simultaneously stay free of all definitions. Tommo does not finally reject the Typees; he flees them. Melville had not yet developed the ironic distance that would enable him to handle his narratives of a younger, more naive self.[21] There are times when Melville seems like James Baldwin's David, spending his life, "having run so far, so hard, across the ocean even, only to find myself brought up short before the bulldog in my own backyard."[22] Typee was a Paradise that evoked both desire and fear—a fear even that desire might be fulfilled—and that could only achieve its purity when seen from afar, in the long retrospect of Melville's life. The "enviable isles" of the early novels became those of the later poems, the islands of memory, purified by time and washed free of fear. They could finally only be attained in death. That, of course, would be the story, and the burden, of *Billy Budd*.

The sense of *Typee*'s incompleteness that many readers feel comes from the inadequate resolution of the novel's own inner dynamics. There are, as we have seen, two journeys involved: the journey on board ship (the childhood world of the "Dolly") and the journey from the ship to the interior of the island. Since the novel effectively ends with the return of Tom to the ship, it is clear that the second of these is the real "plot" of the novel; and yet the novel encompasses both. But the two plots are inherently opposed, since one is undertaken under the rule of the Captain, and the other is undertaken in opposition to the Captain. As Toby acts as the guide to the island, one is led to expect that Marnoo will act as a second guide to the spiritual center of the island. But Tom, along with Melville perhaps, was unable to follow him into that "sacred grove," which seems to involve partaking of human flesh: the sexual taboos were too strong, and so the novel is strangely aborted. Fear brings us back to our beginnings. But the book's inner logic holds that Tom must continue his journey on the island. If Melville could not yet present a hero capable of doing that, he could at least move to a position where the hero might be appraised for the nature of his behavior. Melville is too close to Tom to know what to make of his deepest feelings.

T W O

Chums: The Search for a Friend

After the South Seas novels, Melville no longer structures his work around the search for a place. It is as if his realization of the inevitable imperfections of any society, and his sight of the rapid destruction of the Marquesas as Western influence was introduced, made him turn to an apparently surer basis of support for the wandering Hero: friendship. As we have seen, Melville attaches great significance in the South Seas narratives to the concept of *tayo*, and the later novels attempt to find a place for a similar expression of friendship within Western society. The question in *Redburn* and *White-Jacket* is whether friendship can exist in the world of the ship. *Redburn*'s answer is bleaker than that of *White-Jacket*, although *Redburn* is also far more explicitly devoted to the subject of friendship and sexuality. The failure of friendship in *Redburn*, although based on social custom and prejudice, is ultimately expressed in Redburn's own actions of betrayal: it is his behavior which seems to assert the inability of friendship to offer a real alternative. The novel of initiation, as it has often been called, thus concludes with Redburn's acceptance of the very fallen values he has observed throughout his journey. *White-Jacket* is far closer to the more directly political world of *Typee*: it is an angry denunciation of naval practices, especially flogging, and of the Articles of War. It is in many ways a reform tract, and it uses as the ground of its appeal to a better instinct the figure of Jack Chase, one of Melville's most superb Dark Strangers and one who, far more than the figures of *Typee*, introduces the ethical function of the Stranger. *White-Jacket* portrays the special friendships that can flourish on board ship—Melville terms the practice "chummying"—

but it makes it clear that they exist only within the oppressive structure of a system that is opposed to all the values they may embody. *White-Jacket* is one of Melville's implicitly revolutionary novels, one that, like *Billy Budd*, wonders what would happen if the "people" ever recognized the potential inherent in themselves.

Redburn: "So Singular a Couple"

After the completion of his first three novels, Melville never returned to the theme of the island paradise, except as it influences *Moby-Dick* and as it determines the extraordinary form of his nostalgic poems. Nonetheless the abandonment of the South Seas as a motif of a return to Eden does not mean that the quest-romance structure is abandoned: instead it is internalized.[1] The dual structure of *Redburn* illustrates this change.[2] The first half of *Redburn* is concerned with the journey of the young Redburn from New York to Liverpool: it is a journey to the past, and it results in total disillusion but for the friendship it provides with Harry Bolton. The second half of the novel then shifts radically to take as its subject Harry and his inability to survive (both spiritually and, eventually, literally) aboard ship. The split illustrates the impossibility of fulfilling the dream of friendship, for it can be located nowhere. Cut off from space and time, it can find its home only in memory.

Wellingborough Redburn is marked far more clearly than Tom as an ironic Hero. While Tom's name merely suggests universality, Redburn's suggests fatuousness and preciosity. "Wellingborough," with its clear British ring, is meant to underscore the nature of the journey in *Redburn* as an exploration of the past.[3] At the same time the Hero is as unsuited for his task as, say, J. Alfred Prufrock, another misnamed Hero, is for his. The pompous name prepares the reader for Redburn's naïveté: a naïveté so great that it sometimes strains credulity. But we must recognize that, once again, despite the "facts" of *Redburn*, the novel also takes on many of the qualities of romance: Redburn is a Candide whose innocence strives vainly to survive in a world of harsh reality. Melville's greater irony here makes it easier for the reader to respond to Redburn's adventures, since laughter can accompany pity (whereas tone is always so uncertain in *Typee*), but it should not be understood as a lack of sympathy. Redburn's isolation and loneliness are real, even if the retrospective narration allows Melville to suggest that his own behavior may have brought on some of his suffering. But Redburn, despite the similarities of biography, is not Melville, not even to the degree that Tom is Melville. He fails to recognize the claims of brotherhood and so becomes unworthy of the goal of his quest.

The dual structure of *Redburn* is a part of its elaborate parallelism. In the first half Redburn travels out, from America to Europe; in the second half, Harry travels out, from Europe to America. Wellingborough, the American, has a "British" name; Harry, the Englishman, has an "American" name (that is, a simple, democratic name). Redburn goes in search of "old" England, but never finds the Abbey of Birkenhead or the estate of the earls of Derby; he is forced to conclude that "this boasted England is no older than the state of New York" (p. 159). Harry goes in search of "new" America, but apparently never gets any farther than the docks of New York; Redburn abandons him to Goodwell (good will?), and the land of brotherly love turns out to be as friendless as that he has left. There are numerous other structural parallels (each journey begins with a death, an omen of the failure of the journey) as well as paired characters (in addition to Redburn and Harry, these include the cook and the steward, Larry and "Gun-Deck," and the O'Regan and O'Brien twins) and allusions to Romulus and Remus, Castor and Pollux, and the Horatii and the Curiatii. This overwhelming presence of doubleness in the novel contributes in part to the theme of male friendship—all the doubles are male, and male couples, even if brothers, can serve as figures of erotic desire. But at the same time the balancing of good and evil that is suggested by the twin motif works toward a rejection of whatever idealism lingered from the world of the South Seas. Since Redburn and Harry double each other's journey, it is clear that the journey cannot serve to achieve its goals. If the ideal world is to be found, it must be sought in the self.

The novel is imbued with a sense of failure, and a longing for the world that "might have been." Nowhere is this clearer than in the remarkable chapter 50, in which retrospective speech replaces the ongoing narrative of the other chapters. The Redburn who speaks here is clearly considerably older than the Redburn of the novel, and as such comes closest to merging into Melville himself. Although the narrative will not inform the reader of Harry's death until the final chapter (62), the narrator here steps forward to address the spirit of Harry in a mood of deep longing and regret. This "soliloquy" brings forth the most poetic language of the book, although it must be remarked that the sections concerned with Harry, or Carlo, are always marked by a shift from a narrative to a lyric mode. The use of the apostrophe, or dramatic address, heightens the passage and makes the narrator's words seem almost spoken to his beloved Harry. Seeking consolation, Redburn cannot find it in the thought of Harry's union with nature: "summer may come, but it is winter" for him.[4] Consolation is found in the power of memory to achieve what Walter Pater would call "subjective immortality":[5] Harry lives as, and because, Redburn can call his "image before me" and "see [him], plain and palpable, as in life" (p. 252). The vision of Harry in the groves of Thessaly, as "a zebra, banding with elks," serves as a transition to the narrative, and Redburn goes on to recall "how they hunted you, Harry, my zebra! those ocean barbarians." The entire passage serves to locate for the reader Harry's death before it actually occurs and thus to heighten the drama of his suffering. If the reader only learned of Harry's fate at the end, he might not take so seriously the "hunting" of the "zebra." The rest of the novel is thus imbued with the spirit of loss, and that loss is specifically attributed, in extraordinary imagery, to intolerance and barbarism. It was Newton Arvin who first called attention to this remarkable passage. He connected the depiction of Harry's "equivocal" nature to Shakespeare's Sonnet 20 ("A woman's face with Nature's own hand painted / Hast thou, the master-mistress of my passion"), which Melville marked in his copy of Shakespeare, and asked, "Did he find in this poem an expression of the same ambiguous emotion, the same perplexed attraction, he may once have felt for a young English ne'er-do-well?"[6] Arvin goes astray, I think, in looking for a specific biographical model for the passage, just as his discretion in presenting this argument (perhaps necessary in 1950) leads him away from the central issue. For the elegiac address to the spirit of Harry Bolton does not express "ambiguous emotion" (although "ambiguous" seems to be serving here as a code word) or perplexity. It is unambiguous and unperplexed in its loving memory of a man who has been destroyed for his otherness. What is sad about this passage is that it can only be conceived as a memorial address, when any possibility of the translation of its love into physical expression is past. What makes the passage remarkable, and unlike other such memorials, is the joining together of loss and desire for reunion with the political theme of the outsider destroyed, of difference as the source of victimization. Such a passage is an essential indication of a shift from a concept of male friendship totally consistent with a social world and a concept of homosexuality seen as a fundamental violation of the social order.

Redburn sets out on his journey motivated by the romantic dreams that are produced in him by the relics of his father's journeys—engravings, books, and even a glass ship. But here again there is doubling, for the daydreams of the boy are balanced by a splenetic resolve to flee a world that has already proved deceptive. *Redburn* begins in a state of melancholy that anticipates Ishmael's: "Cold, bitter cold as December, and bleak as its blasts, seemed the world then to me" (p. 10). Leaving home is an expulsion from Eden, and nature seems sympathetically to reflect his own dark state of the soul: "It was early on a raw, cold, damp morning toward the end of spring, and the world was before me . . . " (p. 11). The echo of the conclusion of *Paradise Lost* underscores the narrator's departure from innocence into the world of experience. However, experience leads not to an understanding of a shared responsibility for mankind, although Redburn attempts to assert this in the Launcelott's-Hey episode, but to a fatalistic washing of the hands. The Redburn of the conclusion of the novel, as we shall see, is more another Cain than a second Adam.

Cities, like ships, are places of corruption in which childish illusions are quickly lost, and those in authority serve only to deceive the innocent. Redburn's New York is an anticipation both of the Captain's treachery and of the miseries of Liverpool. Although Redburn is treated well by the Joneses, he will be cheated by the pawnbroker as by the Captain. The depiction of the pawnbroker, although apparently drawn from anti-Semitic stereotypes, serves to stress the hostility and strangeness of the world. The pawnbrokers live off human misery, and the visits Redburn makes to their shops give him an inkling of a poverty and desperation that far exceeds his own. The pawnbroker's Jewishness only emphasizes his role of patriarchal authority; it is above all the women and children who suffer and the men who go about their business. By drawing on the traditional figure of the Jewish pawnbroker, Melville can connect the abuse of authority to a Hebrew tradition of vengeance that is reborn in the moral self-righteousness of the women in Liverpool about the death of the unmarried Betsey Jennings and her children. Like the Christian clergymen who refuse admission to the poor, the Jewish figures represent a betrayal of a religious tradition. They are fathers who have abandoned their children in the service of gold.[7]

The Captain is another false father. He has two different identities, one for the city and one for the ship. They include not only separate sets of clothes but even dyed hair for land only. The naive Redburn believes that the Captain's apparent good manners when he was engaging Redburn will translate into some cordiality on shipboard; but here he ignores the fundamentally hierarchical nature of the ship that prevents any human relationship from developing between ranks. Although Captain Riga, in his authoritarian rule and duplicity, has some of the attributes of the tyrannical captain, Melville shifts the structural pattern slightly in this work by the introduction of the figure of Jackson. Jackson will lend many of his traits to Captain Ahab in *Moby-Dick*, but also to the master-at-arms, Claggart, in *Billy Budd*. Although merely an ordinary seaman, Jackson is characterized by many of the same elements as the Captains, and he is regarded by the other sailors as if he were in a position of authority. "They stand in mortal fear of him" and recognize him as "a tyrant over better men than himself" (p. 59). He represents the tyranny of the democratic hero, a tyranny as great as that of the aristocratic ruler, as Melville increasingly believed.[8] In the failure of the men ever to agree to rebel against Jackson, Melville depicts the self-destructiveness and cowardice that lie at the base of political inaction. It is clear that the men could rebel against Jackson, but they do not. Indeed those he abuses most do most for him. This failure of the men to resist unjust authority is a theme that is important in *White-Jacket*, *Moby-Dick*, and *Billy Budd*.

The analysis of Jackson's own behavior is interesting, as well, since it demonstrates Melville's growing interest in the psychological portrait (almost totally absent from the South Seas novels). Jackson's hatred has its source in envy, above all the envy this consumptive dying man feels for the healthy young men around him. He "eyes" Redburn with "such malevolence," because he is "young and handsome"; he "abuses" the Belfast sailor "because of his great strength and fine person, and particularly because of his red cheeks" (pp. 58–59). He despises in others what he lacks in himself; and if this difference is presented essentially in terms of health, there is enough suggestion of physical beauty to provide an erotic undercurrent, one that will be taken up again by Melville in *Billy Budd* and made the basis for Claggart's hatred of Billy. Signs of that sexual vengeance are already unmistakable in *White-Jacket*. In *Redburn* the idea of a self-feeding hatred is suggested through the name and description of Jackson. The name is a deliberate allusion to "General Jackson of New Orleans" of whom he claims to be "a near relation" (p. 57), and yet he is constantly described in terms that echo white perceptions of the North American Indian. Redburn reports, "He was a horrid desperado; and like a wild Indian, whom he resembled in his tawny skin and high cheek bones, he seemed to run a muck at heaven and earth" (p. 104). At once Indian-hater and Indian, soldier and victim, he is the perfect figure for a violence that is self-generated and self-perpetuating, just as Indian and white in North America continued to fight to avenge the other's inhuman acts.[9]

Jackson is presented as a spirit of negation; he argues at length "that there was nothing to be believed; nothing to be loved, and nothing worth living for" (p. 104). If the tyranny of his authority makes him a double of the Captain, the darkness of his soul makes him also a double of Redburn himself, whose deep melancholy as well comes from his human isolation and lovelessness (Redburn says of himself, "I found myself a sort of Ishmael in the ship, without a single friend or companion; and I began to feel a hatred growing up in me against the whole crew—so much so, that I prayed against it, that it might not master my heart completely, and so make a fiend of me, something like Jackson" [p. 62]). Here again Melville's growing psychological interest is evident; in these depictions of isolation and hatred, he strives to understand how hatred has its source, not so much in innate evil, as in the frustrations that follow upon the failure of love. Jackson's nihilism, Melville suggests, is but the externalization of the emotional state of a man who has found nothing to believe, nothing to love, and nothing to live for. In that way we are all capable of becoming "fiends," Satan being in some sense but Christ's unloved brother.

In a novel so concerned with the theme of brotherhood, it is striking that so little real brotherhood exists. As we have already seen, the authority of the Captain and the hierarchy of the ship act as daily reminders of the denial of brotherhood. Jackson, unloved, becomes a monster of denial and hatred, thus perishing alone, his plunge into the sea a final dramatic presentation of his overwhelming concentration in the self. His very consumption, of which he is presumed to be dying, is merely the metaphor for the way in which he is consumed by hatred. Lacking the nurture of love, he wastes away. Indeed, it should be remarked in general that Melville makes frequent use of food as a metaphor for love. Tom and Toby seem to be about to starve on the meager food they bring from the ship, until they reach the Typees. *There* is copious food, of course, that both nourishes but ultimately frightens Tom into his escape—fleeing as if from love itself. Redburn has nothing to eat for several days before going to sea, and his hunger is a manifestation of his isolation. Once on ship, he cannot eat because he has not known enough to bring his own utensils, and the others refuse to share their meals. The Captain cheats the steerage passengers out of the food that is supposed to be provided for them. And, of course, no one but Redburn will provide any food for the starving family in Launcelott's-Hey. But that food comes too late to save them; they have already been condemned to death of starvation by a society that refuses to take responsibility for its brothers and sisters. (The starvation of the mother and her children and the indifference of everyone around them anticipates the similar theme presented in "Bartleby, the Scrivener"—there Bartleby, like the mother, chooses not to eat.)

It is significant that the one passage of triumphant brotherhood is presented in terms that are at once political and sexual. In chapter 33, the second chapter of the second half of the book, Melville offers a view of the Liverpool harbor in order to present the ships of the various nations alongside each other. Each ship, he says, "is an island," echoing Donne, but the dock as a whole is "an epitome of the world." The ships' masts are made of wood from all the nations and so form "a grand parliament": the idea was far more astonishing in the 1840s than it may appear in our time. But this political symbol of union is quickly turned toward the sexual, for "all climes and countries embrace; and yardarm touches yardarm in brotherly love" (p. 165). The visionary conceit is a moving image of universal affection; and the touching of the yardarms adds a startlingly sexual undercurrent, when we recall that "yard" is slang for the penis.[10] The idea, on both its levels, is worthy of Whitman, and indeed there are several similarly visionary democratic passages throughout Melville's work that remind us of Whitman's sense of a democratic future based on manly (or "adhesive") love.[11] While it is true that Melville almost always balances his visions with a far darker view of human nature that seems likely to render them impossible of achievement, it should be remembered that, like Whitman, he was capable of imagining such a future, if not of seeing how to achieve it. Melville is often thought of as being antidemocratic[12] because of his apparent nostalgia for a *haut-bourgeois* childhood and his hatred of the mob, but his works are marked deeply by a democratic conviction along with a cynical (or haughty) view of the people's unwillingness to fulfill their democratic aspirations.[13] His view of political brotherhood and his view of sexual brotherhood are thus linked: Melville can see their potential for realization, but he continues to doubt that it will ever be achieved. As men fail to love each other on the personal level, they will also fail to love each other on the political level. Melville concludes his chapter on brotherly love in a fashion so visionary ("Then shall the curse of Babel be revoked, a new Pentecost come . . . ") that we realize that any hope for the achievement of brotherhood must await the millennium.

Any romance of brotherly love must be played off, for Melville, against the backdrop of a rigid authority. Captains, Melville reminds us, although "fathers to their crew," are "severe and chastising fathers, fathers whose sense of duty overcomes the sense of love, and who every day, in some sort, play the role of Brutus, who ordered his son away to execution" (p. 67). The theme of the father sacrificing his son for the sake of "duty" remained with Melville until the end of his life, as one can see from *Billy Budd*. If fatherhood is the way of seeing the Captain in personal terms, in larger, more political terms he is a "despot" and a "Czar of Russia" (p. 300) to the emigrants on board his ship. Melville rarely fails to connect the different kinds of authority, since they are the expression of the same thing, on different levels. In both *Redburn* and *White-Jacket* the Captains remain figures of injustice, but relatively distant from the action. The process that begins in *Redburn* of substituting a satanic destroyer for the Captain is continued in *White-Jacket* and *Billy Budd*, but in *Moby-Dick* the role of the Captain and that of the destroyer are joined. Ahab is given some of the attributes of Jackson, especially in his dark, inverted Prometheanism: "Jackson's would have been the face to paint for the doomed vessel's figurehead, seamed and blasted by lightning" (p. 275). (It is perhaps worth recalling the importance of the blasted tree in Romantic pictorial iconography.)[14] Ahab is presented as both Captain and destroyer, although the theme of sexual jealousy is absent. It is in *Moby-Dick* alone, of course, that a male couple is actually presented and not merely proposed as a possibility. Fedallah apparently takes over what is left of Jackson's role. In *Billy Budd*, the pattern returns to the original distinction between Captain and destroyer, and the two become part of a new configuration of three, along with the Handsome Sailor. There is no young Hero like that of the earlier novels and so no one to form a bond with Billy, except Claggart and his bond of hatred (formed, like Jackson's, out of thwarted love).

Redburn's treatment of the failures of civilization is more complex than that of *Typee*. Larry, the whaleman, expresses the primitivist position in a comic version. "What's the use of bein' *snivelized*?" he asks Redburn, "snivelized chaps only learns the way to take on 'bout life, and snivel" (p. 100). The mock-dialect is part of the comic effect, of course, and one can often use a rural bumpkin voice as a way of presenting truths otherwise unavailable; but Larry is balanced by the man-of-war's man, "Gun-Deck," who has "seen the civilized world, and loved it; found it good and a comfortable place to live in" (p. 101). The use of the doubles here makes it almost impossible to establish a position of Melville's, either for or against civilization; there is something to be said for both sides of the argument. But if nowhere in the novel does Melville establish a position on the question, the structure of the work itself indicates a far greater concern with the failures of civilization than with those of primitive life. Liverpool, which Redburn looks forward to as a representative of the height of English civilization, turns out to be poor, unattractive, and morally corrupt. Harry Bolton, the representative of a "high" civilization, is a troubled and finally destroyed individual who seems to lack a fundamental sense of place. He is unable to function in the "primitive" world of the ship. And Redburn's one excursion into the English countryside brings him up against "man-traps and spring-guns," unmistakable signs of a corruption of bucolic charm by the values of property. The doubling of Harry and Carlo, the two romantic objects of Redburn's attention and the two figures of the artist, serves to point up the greater aptitude for survival of the "primitive" Carlo over the "civilized" Harry. Insofar as civilization means artifice, it represents a corruption of an original purity of form: thus Melville's Romantic neoclassicism leads him to identify the "primitive" of his time with a pure classicism of the Greeks.

As we can say that Melville's ideal in *Typee* is an intermediate figure, such as Marnoo, who is at once barbarian and civilized, Polynesian and Greek, so it seems that in general Melville looked toward such figures of integration. Redburn and Harry, the innocent American and the corrupt Englishman, would need to come together as a couple in order to achieve that harmony of being. Carlo seems to come close to achieving it within himself. Melville's attitude toward civilization, and overcivilization, is an important factor in understanding his attitude toward his homosexual, or potentially homosexual, characters. Harry is descended from the literary tradition of the fop. In his Restoration origins, such a character has no homosexual overtones; in fact suggestions of overdressing, wearing perfume, and so forth, are linked to an undue interest in women. It is in line with this tradition that Melville can present effeminate characters who are clearly heterosexual, such as Selvagee in *White-Jacket*, since "effeminate" connoted too much liking for women rather than being too much like a woman. Melville clearly disliked effeminate men; like Whitman his literary sexual ideal involves a love between two men, and not a man and a boy, or a man and a pseudo-woman. The effeminate man was the overcivilized man, one who had adopted the values of civilization (i.e., woman) over those of the primitive (i.e., man). The ideal therefore becomes an androgyny that represents the integration of the values of civilization and the primitive, or of female and male. This androgyny should not be confused with effeminacy; for Melville, androgyny indicates self-sufficiency and wholeness, whereas effeminacy indicates weakness, indulgence, and partialness.

It may well be that Harry Bolton was a late addition to Melville's conception of *Redburn*, as has been argued.[15] Certainly nothing in the first half of the book prepares us for his appearance, let alone for the startling emotional role he is to play. His presence in the work as it now stands transforms an otherwise conventional sea voyage into an exploration of the self and a profound study in human relationships. Harry Bolton is the means by which Melville can present the darker side of Redburn's own personality, and the means by which he can dramatize Redburn's ultimate refusal to recognize his place in the brotherhood of man. Harry's introduction into the narrative is handled in a striking manner. Redburn has made his excursion into the country, where he learns that the pastoral is no longer possible in a world of property rights, and he has had his blissful meal with the three "adorable charmers" whose beauty, he claims, has kept him a bachelor ever since. He goes to sleep that night "dreaming of red cheeks and roses" and awakens the next morning to meet Harry Bolton. The episode with the three charmers is a piece of hackwork, drawn directly from the sentimental romance; its only function here is to prepare us for the erotic world into which Harry will enter. For it is Harry who offers Redburn the opportunity of real sustenance, and it is Harry whose beauty will trouble Redburn until his death. The initial description of Harry is surprisingly frank about his androgynous appearance:

> He was one of those small, but perfectly formed beings, with curling hair, and silken muscles, who seem to have been born in cocoons. His complexion was a mantling brunette, feminine as a girl's; his feet were small; his hands were white; and his eyes were large, black, and womanly; and poetry aside, his voice was as the sound of a harp. [p. 216]

Although "womanly" or "feminine," Harry is never effeminate. His physical attributes are assumed to be those of the aristocracy, but they never prevent him from being forceful and active. His voice like "a harp" associates him with David, the biblical musician/charmer and lover of a king's son (1 Sam. 16:21–23; 18:1–9), while his darkness links him to Toby and Marnoo. Like them he is without origins, "early left an orphan" (p. 217). Redburn's response to Harry is enthusiastic: "I now had a comrade. . . . Harry. . . shared with me his purse and his heart," but Redburn is unable to give himself entirely to this new friend. Troubled by Harry's "imperial reminiscences of high life," which are of course but the echoes of his own reminiscences of a gentle birth and high relations, he "hold[s] back" his "whole soul," and this to his regret, for "in its loneliness, [my soul] was yearning to throw itself into the unbounded bosom of some immaculate friend" (p. 223). Redburn's scruples are excessive, since, as we have said, Harry's legends of his past are not that different from Redburn's own, and since the desire for an "immaculate" friend is impossible to realize in the fallen world of human life. The connotations of the word "immaculate" suggest as well an element of sexual fastidiousness, whether on the part of Melville himself or only of Redburn is difficult to say with certainty at this remove. It is certainly in Redburn's character to continue to set himself up as morally superior even when confronted with someone who in almost every way corresponds to his desires. Such caution allows him to keep his hands even whiter than Harry's.

The trip to London that Harry and Redburn undertake together is one of the least successful of all the episodes in the novel. One reason for its failure may well be that Melville in fact never went to London on the trip

that formed the basis for this novel and thus was unable to write accurately of the city. This would explain the total absence of any sense of
observed detail. On the other hand, Melville frequently used literary
sources for his descriptions and could easily have employed them here. A
more significant reason for the weakness of this section is Melville's unwillingness, or inability, to be specific about the world he is attempting to
suggest. Some of that reluctance may be owing to a sense of social propriety, but since that frequently does not prevent Melville from making
sexual allusions it is hard to see why it should have been so strong here.
My own suggestion is that Aladdin's Palace is at once a luxurious gambling den and a male brothel. Like Oscar Wilde in *Dorian Gray* forty years
later, Melville chose to create a sense of generalized sinfulness, hinting at
gambling and drugs, as well as homosexuality, in order to avoid specific
presentations of homosexual activity. Wilde, however, had been to such
places and could certainly have described one had he dared. Melville seems
unable to, perhaps because he himself had had no such experience and
literary treatments could provide only the general air of mystery and decadence. Everything is false there (including Harry, disguised with whiskers
and mustache): trompe-l'oeil colonnades, ceilings painted with "mimic
grapes" and sculpted "vine-boughs." It is a world of total artifice, from
which nature is forever banished, present only in replica. Melville's coy
reference to the pictures of Pompeii and others, many details of which are
apparently inaccurate, is designed to introduce the sexual element into the
scene; at least one of them depicts a (male-female) act of fellatio.[16] Part of
the reticence in describing this scene comes from the voice of Redburn;
since he never really understands where he is or what transpires there, it is
natural that his account of it should be vague and cast in his usual coy
terms. But if Melville wanted his readers to understand more than Redburn does, he could have provided clearer indications. As it is, he had no
idea how to depict the life of a decadent aristocrat and little idea what a
gambling den or a brothel looked like. He tried to suggest them in a way
that might provoke horror and a simultaneous attraction.

Because of the unreality of this episode, it is reasonable to ask whether
we are justified in understanding Harry Bolton as a homosexual.[17] My
view is that the very awkwardness of the scene confirms Melville's attempt
to deal with material that was both foreign and embarrassing to him. The
mystery is hardly necessary if we are to understand Harry as a simple
gambler. I believe that we are justified in calling Harry homosexual for
several reasons: for his physical appearance, which, although derived from
earlier nonhomosexual models was changing over the course of this period into a physical confirmation of homosexuality; for the joy with which

Redburn responds to him and to the time they spend together; for the intensity with which Redburn (or Melville) mourns him; and for the way Melville depicts him on ship, a victim of the crew for his difference, a depiction that culminates in the metaphor of the "zebra." If I am right, there is an enormous difference between this novel and the earlier *Typee*. *Typee* could be considered a homosexual novel because the most convincing presentation of eros is located in a man and because friendship is invested with considerable social power. But nothing about it suggests to us a world in which homosexual desire is fulfilled. *Redburn*, by taking its setting to England, makes that fulfillment possible, if artistically difficult. *Redburn* also breaks new ground by beginning to consider homosexuality in its social context and by identifying the homosexual as the victim of an arbitrary code of social behavior. By locating homosexuality in the world, *Redburn* has the potential to transform it from dream to reality. It is that potential that is so frightening in *Redburn* and that leads in the end to Redburn's flight, a conclusion that links this work structurally to *Typee* and Tom's flight.

In the world of ships, where Melville recognizes the existence of homosexual practices, the friendship of Redburn and Harry can exist; but what place could it have on land? This is the problem that the novel confronts at its conclusion, and it is precisely the impossibility of imagining a relationship between Redburn and Harry on land that leads Melville to his somewhat abrupt ending. There are certainly good reasons in Redburn's character as already presented for us to imagine him capable of betraying Harry, but I do not think we can overlook the difficulties that the developing plot of Redburn and Harry would have presented. At this point the character's weakness seems to coincide with the author's artistic (and perhaps personal) difficulty.

While on board ship, Harry has a power that can almost overcome the hatred of the crew members for his difference, represented most clearly in his inability to climb the masts. It is tempting to see in the particular failure a sexual difference: since the masts themselves are taken in the novel as sexual objects, it seems likely that the ability to climb a mast is taken as a sign of virility, and Harry's failure confirms the mistaken idea that homosexuals are less virile than other men. He possesses an extraordinary power of song, one that enables the author to liken him to Orpheus, whose music could charm the savage beasts; when Harry sings, the sailors are "charmed leopards and tigers" (p. 278). Orpheus is the mythic figure of the poet, and so Harry's fate is shown by Melville to be characteristic of the artist in modern society: Melville's own relative failure as an artist led him to increasing pessimism about the fate of the artist, as "Bartleby" or

Pierre shows, and *Redburn* already responds to Melville's disappointment at the reception of *Mardi*. But Orpheus is also the mythic introducer of homosexuality, according to Ovid, and he is destroyed for his "crime."[18] Orpheus represents a Dionysian force of joyous celebration and a power of love, killed by the coldness of the world.[19] That Melville made conscious reference to Orpheus is confirmed by his use of the theme again in *Billy Budd*, where it serves to underline the irony of Vere's claim to use Orpheus in his defense. Like Narcissus, whom Melville uses in *Moby-Dick*, Orpheus is a culture hero of a subversive sort, one who speaks for the constant need to reaffirm the self and pleasure against a society committed to the extinction of the self through work. The Orphic singer has small enough place in England; what place can there be for him in the new commercial America that Melville depicts? Singing and writing can only be made profitable by turning into singing in the salons of the rich or writing as a copyist (scrivener) or clerk—in other words, only by betraying their Orphic origins and making them into acts in the service of something else. Creativity seems doomed. There is as little room for art as there is for the sensitive spirit; one must apparently be hardened or die.

Harry's characteristic form is the pastoral, and the form in which he is honored by Melville is the pastoral elegy. His voice, we are told, "meandered and tinkled through the words of a song, like a musical brook that winds and wantons by pied and pansied margins" (p. 277). But the shepherd is cast out of Arcady and into the world of the industrial city. In that world such a pastoral can only be an appeal to a long-lost and perhaps only dreamed-of world of the past; this would become a frequent motif of Melville's own poems. Like the innocent homosexuality of the pastoral transformed into the corrupt world of a decadent Rome, the world that Harry sings from and of seems sullied by any contact with reality. Melville's own language grows lyrical as he thinks of Harry: we can see the careful musical structure of that last clause, with its alliterations, assonances, and balanced meter: "*wi*nds and *wa*ntons/by *p*ied and *p*ansied." Music here is both sensual (it "wantons") and disseminal, as it meanders and winds, moving from center to "margins"—like Whitman's place of self-revelation in the first *Calamus* poem. The introduction into *Redburn* of such passages, and particularly of the elegy for Harry in chapter 50, is an indication of Melville's shift toward the symphonic structure of *Moby-Dick*. There, as we shall see, shifts in voice indicate changes from one mode to another, and rhetoric becomes an expression of self. The matter-of-fact reportorial tone remains, along with the comic self-ironic voice, both present in the earlier works, but they are joined by language that can range from the pastoral to the dramatic. Pastoral is often thought of as a

particularly homosexual form, and in part this may be due to the presence
of homosexual lovers in some of the best-known poems. But there may
also be something that we can think of as homosexual in the very nature of
the form: its nostalgia, its dreaminess, its advocacy of pleasure, and its
freedom from action. Pastoral depicts a world of community among the
disenfranchised, "bound together into a shared life of spirit and emotion
through poetry and love," as Amitai Avi-Ram has recently put it.[20] Whatever the reason, the pastoral interventions in *Redburn* serve to dignify and
to magnify our sense of loss at the failure of love. They add another voice
to the novel's complex narration.

Harry's role as the spirit of music is doubled by the figure of Carlo, the
young Italian musician. Carlo is also beautiful, in a "feminine" way, a
"rich-cheeked, chestnut-haired Italian boy" with "thick clusters of tendril
curls, half overhanging the brows and delicate ears" and a "naked leg [as]
beautiful to behold as any lady's arm; so soft and rounded, with infantile
ease and grace" (p. 247). Like Harry and the other dark, handsome figures, he is fatherless, but in sharp contrast to Harry's aristocratic connections, Carlo is "a poor and friendless son of earth" (p. 248). While Harry
is a singer of the elegant songs of the salon, Carlo is a street musician with
a hand organ. They are thus doubles in terms of both class and race. For,
although Harry's "mantling brunette complexion" makes him in some
sense dark, he is clearly a part of the Western white tradition. Mediterranean cultures, whether Italian or Spanish (Carlo is compared to a Murillo
painting and seems very much like a Caravaggio), are perceived by northern Europeans of the nineteenth century as essentially nonwhite. Carlo is
very much a noble savage, while Harry might better be termed a savage
noble. While Harry is compared above all to Orpheus, Carlo is linked
particularly to Dionysus. Like a wine god, "he might have ripened into
life in a Neapolitan vineyard"; the curls of his hair recall "a classic vase,
piled up with Falernian foliage" (p. 247). Because of his earthiness, Carlo
is loved by the crew and arrives triumphantly in America. As a street
musician, Carlo represents an art that is in touch with the people, a democratic and commercial art that may survive in America when Harry's more
aristocratic traditions must fail.

Carlo is of course hardly a character; there is no interaction between
Redburn and him, or indeed between him and anyone else. He is an
allegorical figure and an erotic image. There is nothing to suggest that
Carlo himself is homosexual, but he clearly represents a figure of homosexual desire. While part of the reason for the distinction between Harry
and Carlo lies in the natures of their art, another reason for their difference, and for the different fates they meet, may lie in the possibilities for

frankness in erotic themes in the nineteenth century. Carlo can safely be introduced as an erotic figure because he is young, foreign, and poor. His youth means that the androgyny depicted in him may be seen as a characteristic of his age and that he may grow into "manhood." Furthermore, the beautiful boy has a long artistic tradition (which Melville calls upon by the Murillo reference) as well as the justification of Greek philosophy (and Melville duly cites Plato in his support). As a foreigner, a Latin, he is assumed to be more feminine and more sensitive than an Anglo-Saxon; hence what would be suspect in Harry can pass without comment in Carlo. Finally, friendship for him as a poor boy can betoken mere charity—Horatio Alger's works are a perfect example of the ability of the Victorian mind to accept as Christian friendship the portrayal of a barely sublimated erotic relationship between an older man and a poor boy. Thus the portrayal of Carlo, especially because it involves no psychological portraiture, poses no real problems for Melville, while that of Harry comes dangerously close to breaking the taboo on the presentation of a homosexual relationship between two Anglo-Saxons of the same class. Such a relegation of the sexual to those outside one's class is intricately related to the antisocial nature of homosexuality itself, and it continued to play a role in the lives of homosexuals themselves well into the twentieth century—think of E. M. Forster's famous remark about wanting to be loved by a man of the lower classes, or J. R. Ackerley's inability to love anyone but working-class boys.[21] It is interesting to note that Melville's reviewers were sometimes troubled by the portrait of Harry—Frederick Hardman, writing in *Blackwood's Edinburgh Magazine*, refers to Harry as a "he-brunette" and "the male brunette" and contrasts the "sentimental effusions" about Harry to the "plain, vigorous, unaffected writing" of other sections of the novel—whereas the complaints about Carlo were always restricted to the stylistic—three different reviews (perhaps copying each other) complain about the "rhapsodies" on Carlo and his music.[22]

The passages on Carlo ought perhaps to have troubled some readers, because they are probably the most extravagant paean to masturbation to have appeared in respectable literature. Several pages are devoted to Carlo's "hand-organ" and its powers of transport. The passage obviously anticipates the "sperm-squeezing" chapter of *Moby-Dick*, but it does not have its political implications. Masturbation as presented in *Redburn* is linked to the imagination and to the power of art to create a world in the mind. As Carlo plays, Redburn himself is moved by the power of sympathy and by a sense of identity. He becomes the object of Carlo's music, no longer a conscious being but instead a vibrating rod, an Aeolian harp, on which sensations can play. The music of Carlo brings Redburn "back" to the

South Seas (where of course only Melville and not Redburn has been): "Turn hither your pensive, morning eyes; and while I list to the organs twain—one yours, one mine—let me gaze fathoms down into thy fathomless eye;—'tis good as gazing down into the great South Sea, and seeing the dazzling rays of the dolphins there" (p. 250). The hand organ has been taken by some critics to be a symbol of the womb—by which they presumably mean the vagina—but I cannot imagine a more misleading interpretation.[23] Whatever a hand organ may look like, its name and its powers make it clear that it is a part of Carlo that he can play with his hand and so transport himself, and his listeners, to any mood and any place. The hand organ is the penis, and Carlo's music is the internal imaginative music of fantasy. It is the transport of sexual ecstasy. It is important to note that this chapter is subversive not merely because of its suggestions of sexuality, but more precisely because it praises masturbation as a kind of self-sufficient sexuality. As Carlo puts it, "it is my only friend, poor organ! it sings to me when I am sad, and cheers me." In the context of the nineteenth-century crusade against masturbation, Melville's passage takes on crucial importance as an assertion of the values of the freely roving imagination and of a sexuality that is not harnessed to production. Masturbation, the Carlo chapters suggest, is like music in that it offers nothing but the ability to move our minds and offer us an infinite variety of pleasure of the mind. Music, Walter Pater would soon explain, was the art toward which all others aspired, precisely because of its non-linear and non-narrative nature.[24] Thus it is not surprising that Melville's chapters on Carlo should be written in the lyric mode; they are an astonishing anticipation of late nineteenth-century techniques of subverting the novel, as in Huysmans's *A Rebours*, or Wilde's adaptation of that manner in *Dorian Gray*. The catalog of pleasures, like the rhapsody or improvisation on a theme, become techniques for working against the fundamental structure of the novel, action > climax, as courtship > marriage. All of these chapters are, from one point of view, digressions in Melville's novel about Redburn's journey to Liverpool and back; but Melville was increasingly using the digression as the center of interest. *Moby-Dick* would become a novel composed primarily of digressions, in which narrative development took on a secondary role. So the enumerated visions of Carlo's hand organ are digressions, a succession of pleasures rather than a progression toward a single climax.

When the ship arrives in New York, Carlo does not join the others in looking at the land; instead he is seen "leaning over, in a reverie, against the side, my Carlo gazed down into the calm, violet sea, as if it were an eye that answered his own" (p. 298). The position of the gazer in reverie links

Carlo to Toby and Ishmael, and reinforces his role as the masturbator/ dreamer. The image is also one of completion: the eye of the sea seems to "answer" his own, and Carlo remarks that he finds in the sea of the New World what he had known in the sky of the Old (thus anticipating the sea/sky union at the end of *Moby-Dick*). Because Carlo is associated with these figures of completeness, it is not surprising that he should arrive triumphantly in the harbor. The woods and fields glow "with a glorious green," signaling hope and a new spring for this chthonic deity. And while most of the passengers are obliged to stay on board, Carlo is rowed ashore, "seated in the stern of the boat, his organ before him, and something like 'Hail Columbia' his tune" (pp. 300, 301). The future is not so hopeful for Harry. Although he and Redburn do go ashore together, and a chapter is devoted to them "arm in arm," Redburn's betrayal spoils whatever pleasure Harry may have anticipated. Although the two have spoken about a future together in America, Redburn soon leaves Harry alone; when he returns he seems surprised to observe "a marked change in his countenance," but he comments blithely, "He was a creature of the suddenest impulses" (p. 304). The change, of course, is in Redburn more than in Harry, and it must come as a particular shock for the reader who has already read Redburn's long lament for Harry, for whose loss he will "never . . . be comforted" (p. 252). The Redburn of the end of the novel is as ironic a depiction as the naive figure of the opening.

Although James Miller has argued that Redburn has acquired "a new self-confidence—the poise not of the self-sustained and isolated man, but that of the man whose isolation has been penetrated, and who has discovered in its stead the sustaining warmth of strong human relationships . . . the love of the young comrade Bolton,"[25] he confuses what the dynamics of the novel as romance quest for friendship seem to call for and what Melville's ironic treatment actually portrays. Certainly the novel makes us want to believe that Redburn will lose his pretensions with his innocence and find a personal love to correspond to his awakened social conscience, but something makes him veer away from that ending, whether an innate pessimism, a dislike for the sentimental romance conventions that would then come into play (are we to imagine Harry and Redburn in domestic harmony?—this would be the problem E. M. Forster faced in *Maurice*), or an inability to imagine a fulfilled homosexual love. The novel concludes in fact with an ironic portrayal of Redburn's "initiation into guilt," as Bruce Franklin has phrased it.[26] His abandonment of Harry is as criminal an act as that of the police who look the other way and claim that the dying family in Liverpool are not under their jurisdiction. Redburn has other business to attend to; and so he simply salves his conscience by putting

Harry in the hands of Goodwell who "will do his best for you" (p. 310). Harry is not fooled by this, and neither is the reader. Redburn's denial of responsibility makes him the murderer of Harry Bolton. When the sailor who tells him of the manner of Harry's death (crushed between a ship and a whale) asks Redburn, "Harry Bolton was not your Brother?" (p. 312), he echoes God's question to Cain, "Where is Abel thy brother?" and Cain's answer, "I know not: Am I my brother's keeper?" By betraying Harry, Redburn denies the brotherhood the novel has established as the highest good. If he cannot be true to a single friend, how can he be true to his universal responsibilities?

Redburn thus concludes by pointing up the connections between personal friendship and the brotherhood of man. The inability to sustain the one provides no basis for the other. Bonds between nations will only be firmly made when personal affection and love are allowed to flourish, on land as on sea. *Redburn* is an astonishing novel that portrays the possibility of a renewed spirit of human relations through the recognition of friendship and sexuality between men. But, although it can portray that possibility, it cannot realize it. Human nature, Melville seems to suggest, aided by social convention, will work against the kind of affection that comes so near to prevailing in *Redburn*. The novel's ending demonstrates that an actual Captain is not necessary as an obstacle to the union of Hero and Stranger; for the Hero himself is capable of accepting and imposing the Captain's values and so betraying himself as well as his friend.

White-Jacket: "A Brother-Band, Hand in Hand"

If *Redburn* is a novel of regret, *White-Jacket* is a novel of anger. It is as if Melville had decided to explore the implications of that extraordinary scene near the end of *Redburn*, when the crew pay their final respect to the Captain by offering him the salute of a row of asses. The gesture is only that and it makes no difference in the Captain's behavior, but it may have suggested to Melville the idea of exploring the social unity of the crew and its potential revolutionary force. The crew in *White-Jacket* is ultimately defeated, but it has discovered the value of comradeship and in its union seems to offer hope for the future. As in *Redburn*, the Hero is isolated from the rest of the crew, and his isolation is marked off by a garment: the red shooting jacket of *Redburn*, and the white jacket of the later novel. Both garments act as visible signs of spiritual difference and can become the occasion for social ridicule and ostracism. The white jacket offers the possibility of a new life as well; it is, we learn in the first chapter, "white as a shroud" (p. 3) so that the narrator's emergence from it at the end of the novel marks a rebirth, like Ishmael's survival in the coffin of Queequeg. Less specific about the nature of friendship and sexuality, *White-Jacket* is able to be far more optimistic about a democratic, brotherly future.

White-Jacket is Melville's most political novel, and its political critique is far-reaching in its implications. For Melville develops here the connections he uses so successfully in *Moby-Dick*: the connections between political authority, religious authority, racism, militarism, and rationalism, and their necessary suppression of all human affection. Although the novel's explicit goals seem to be the abolition of flogging and the modification of the Articles of War, its actual goals go much further by questioning an entire system of authority. The novel comes just short of advocating actual revolution; Melville veers away from this implication at the end, perhaps frightened by the logic of his own argument, but also convinced as always that the exploitation of individuals and the deprivation of their liberty is partly their own doing. *White-Jacket* is above all a call to resist authority and to make oneself free.

Shipboard authority is located in three figures, the commodore, the captain, and the master-at-arms. The commodore is the most remote, compared with a statue of Jupiter, "silent and stately" (p. 6). Although playing almost no part in the daily life of the ship, he represents the highest, most inscrutable, level of authority. His virtually divine nature makes him inaccessible, and he suffers from a profound loneliness, along with a shoulder wound from an earlier campaign. That wound and that isolation do something to humanize him (Melville would develop the concept of the agony of the isolation of power in *Moby-Dick* and *Billy Budd*), and Melville even suggests that had the commodore had some of "the rare good fellows" into his cabin for an evening of drinking, his "ancient wound" would "heal up at once" (p. 22). Lacking brotherhood and affection, the commodore develops into a brooding, distant figure.

The Captain is less remote, but more to be feared, since he exercises his power, and in a most arbitrary way. He is compared with Henry VIII, "as kingly in his cabin as Harry on his throne" (p. 23). The comparison is not an accidental one, owing merely to size and appetite; for Melville reminds his readers that ships are monarchies and hence essentially at variance with American political ideals. The most awful element of the Captain's power is his control over the floggings. They are an exercise of "omnipotent authority" (p. 135) designed to humiliate and assert power as well as to inflict pain. They do nothing to alter behavior except instill fear in the weakest—the hardened criminal types seem indifferent to the punishment—and they bear but the faintest resemblance to justice. They violate the Christian injunction to forgiveness: Melville reminds us of this by giving Captain Claret the satanic line, "I would not forgive God Almighty!," in response to Peter's cries and pleas. They represent the domination of an arbitrary code of justice, in which once again human law and natural law are at odds. For floggings are punishments "for things not essentially criminal, but only made so by arbitrary laws" (p. 138). The clearest example of this arbitrariness (which suggests the way in which an entire penal system has gone beyond—or even against, as we will see in *Billy Budd*—its function of punishing the "essentially," or naturally, criminal) comes in the punishment of the two blacks, Rose-Water and May-Day. These blacks are regularly employed by the Captain in "sports" such as "Head-bumping," a striking anticipation of our modern taste for black boxers killing themselves for the entertainment of a white audience. However, when they once actually fight, after May-Day calls Rose-Water a "nigger," they are flogged at the Captain's order. The episode serves to remind us that although the Captain has favored them and allowed their sportsmanship to give them privileges, they remain his "slaves."

The arbitrariness of punishment is also underscored by the chapter devoted to the midshipmen and the power they hold, since, in a conflict with a sailor, they are presumed never to be wrong. And yet what is to prevent them from accusing a sailor unjustly? Such an incident is alluded to in chapter 52, although Melville feels obliged to be slightly vague about the details that "cannot here be related." Their relation would apparently have to wait for *Billy Budd*, in which sexual jealousy again becomes a motive for unjust punishment. In the incident in *White-Jacket* the midshipman is "apt to indulge at times in undignified familiarities with some of the men, who, sooner or later, almost always suffered from his capricious preferences" (p. 216). In a hierarchical order there can be no justice, since superiors will always be believed over inferiors. And since those superiors have their own superiors, they may in turn avenge themselves for the injustices inflicted on them, not by attacking their superiors but their inferiors. Such relations of power inevitably color any sexual relations that may exist and work against their becoming relations of affection as well; it is important to remember that it is not so much sex that poses a challenge to authority as affection.

If the Captain is arbitrary and unjust, he is not precisely evil. That role is given to the master-at-arms, in another significant anticipation of the patterns to be developed in *Billy Budd*. The master-at-arms is compared with Vidocq, the infamous Paris chief of police who was a notorious criminal and child molester. By this comparison, it is clear that Melville wants us to understand the master-at-arms as the police force of the state, necessarily corrupt and evil, and knowingly used by higher authority as a way of keeping order. Law, as Melville shows, is but a means for the maintenance of power. As Kathleen Keir has put it, law as Melville depicts it is "a support to evil rather than a defense for good, a mere form which satisfies man's need for pattern that simulates order."[27] The evil of the master-at-arms is frightening because it does not look like evil; he is charming and witty, indeed, as Melville says, he could have been "an irreproachable mercantile swindler, circulating in polite society" (p. 187). His smuggling of liquor is therefore not merely a shipboard crime but a sign of all "mercantile" crime, the way in which a society organized around monetary value artificially increases the price of objects to increase businessmen's profits. The master-at-arms is like the white-collar criminal, rarely caught, closely connected to the highest authority, and, if caught, sure to be let off with a very light sentence. The master-at-arms is soon reinstated after his crime is discovered, although his henchmen are flogged and put in irons, and he continues in his office as representative of the law, as apt for his post as, more recently, John Mitchell for his. The maintenance of that authority requires the suppression of particular affections: the military must not allow love to interfere with duty. And so the master-at-arms, when Shenly has died and his friend is mourning him, stands by with his rattan, and "put[s] an end" to such a display of affection. In another passage, a weeping man holds the body of his friend Tom who has just been killed, but the lieutenant orders him to toss "that thing" overboard and leaves him "heart-stricken" (p. 316). Allegiance is owed to authority, not to each other. War must kill all that is decent in its participants.

The ordinary bonds of affection are everywhere denied on board a man-of-war. When Mandeville is brought on board in Rio, he turns out to be a former roommate of the first lieutenant. His mention of their connection, "We had the same state-room. . . . I'm your old chum" does him no good; the lieutenant is an officer and Mandeville is now a common sailor. Thus the lieutenant declares, "If you ever violate the ship's rules, you shall be flogged like any other seaman" (p. 242). An even more disturbing violation of human brotherhood occurs in the subsequent chapter, when Frank discovers that his brother is an officer aboard a storeship in Rio. Out of shame that his brother might see him, "a miserable sailor that any moment may be flogged at the gangway, before his very eyes" (p. 244), Frank is obliged to disguise himself and so avoid meeting the brother. Distance and loneliness become the effect of a hierarchical order that so explicitly denies the brotherhood of man.

Despite the pressures, some affection does persist among the men, if not between men and officers. The death of Shenly is the occasion for Melville's presentation of the bonds of love that can survive even in this inhospitable environment. White-Jacket himself keeps the deathwatch for Shenly, sitting by him all night and fanning his face until death arrives. Kathleen Kier has called attention to the antiheroic nature of this episode; it subverts social (and literary) values by depicting a simple act of affection, "a noble and loving deed, but hardly the stuff about which history is written."[28] Like Whitman a few years later, in his *Calamus* and *Drum-Taps* poems, Melville is suggesting the need for an art that can encompass the nonheroic.[29] The heroic is the mode of the poetry of war; if one is to have a poetry of peace, and of love instead of conquest, its elements must include such apparently insignificant moments. After Shenly's death, Pierre, who had been his "chummy,"[30] "spent much time in tying the neckerchief in an elaborate bow, and affectionately adjusting the white frock and trowsers" (p. 337). But, as we have seen, even this affection, which is directed toward a man who is safely dead (that is, not able to respond to the affection), is interrupted by the forces of "order." Still, Shenly's spirit seems to survive, and indeed to triumph, in the "snow-white, solitary fowl" that ascends just as Shenly's body is dropped into the sea. The scene demonstrates another clear connection to *Billy Budd*; in this case the fact that the novel is explicitly identified with Ovid's *Metamorphoses* (p. 3) requires us to understand that the bird represents a metamorphosis of the spirit of Shenly, like Narcissus reborn as a flower.

If affection is suspect and severely restricted aboard a military ship, sexuality is by no means absent. The most obvious presentation of sexuality occurs in the chapter, "Killing Time," in which it appears that masturbation is one of the principal ways of killing time on board ship. Melville's presentation here is through barely concealed double entendres, which are presented with the gusto that is characteristic of his treatment of the phallic theme. White-Jacket himself is a polisher of brass, which he can bring to a shine equal "to Rogers's best cutlery" (p. 171). Another favored pastime is falling "into as snug a little revery as you can." One of the marines will saunter about, looking at the men, and then "heave a sentimental sigh, and hum to himself 'The girl I left behind me'" (p. 172). If Melville is prepared to allude to masturbation, at least indirectly, he takes a totally different tone with regard to other sexual practices. From "close confinement," he reports, "arise other evils, so direful that they will hardly bear even so much as an allusion. . . . The sins for which the cities of the plain were overthrown still linger in some of these wooden-walled Gomorrahs of the deep" (pp. 375–76). Unless one believes that Melville was simply being hypocritical here, and pretending to a horror he did not feel, it is necessary to pause a moment to consider the implications of this passage and its relationship to what has already been said about Melville's attitude to male friendship and to sexuality. Newton Arvin, who was the first to suggest Melville's fundamental homosexuality, uses this passage to support his view that although Melville was conscious of his feelings, "the possibility that such emotions might have had a sexual undercurrent can only with the utmost rarity, and then fleetingly, have presented itself to his consciousness."[31] Is it possible that Melville, psychologist that he was, can have been so innocent about the human mind? I think we must suppose that Melville was more aware of human motives and behavior than Arvin seems to allow. To the question, Did Melville when writing *White-Jacket* (or later) oppose homosexual practices?, the possibilities then are: that he opposed them then, but changed his mind later, before writing *Moby-Dick*, with its enthusiastic sexuality; that he always opposed homosexual practices and favored only a "Platonic," nonphysical homosexuality; or that he distinguished between buggery or sodomy and homosexuality, opposing the former and approving the latter, which then meant, in effect, mutual masturbation. My view is the last of these: every positive depiction of sexuality in Melville is a depiction of male masturbation, frequently mutual. There is never any portrayal of sexuality involving, as the Victorians put it, penetration. This attitude coincided with many legal definitions that restricted the crime of buggery or sodomy to anal penetration as well as with the widespread Victorian identification of homosexuality and masturbation;[32] it helps to explain a symbolic system in Melville that places so much weight on physical contact and sharing and that views all elements of aggression or penetration negatively as elements of male power. Melville knew that his feelings had a sexual basis, but he wanted that sexuality expressed in a way that for him conveyed mutuality and sharing rather than power and possession; thus for him the love between men was to be expressed through a mutual masturbation that affirmed affection (and reverie) and denied aggression.

The most important figure in *White-Jacket*, and one who brings together a political and a sexual appeal, is Jack Chase. Much attention has been devoted to this figure, especially since Melville later dedicated *Billy Budd* to him. Although there was a real Jack Chase, Melville seems to have depicted him as the "Handsome Sailor," a character type that had been developed in a number of sea novels, including Dana's *Two Years Before the Mast* and Marryat's *Mr. Midshipman Easy*. A study of some of the sources indicates that Melville's borrowings "were shaped . . . so as to enhance the character of Jack Chase . . . [and] increase our impression of Jack's warmth and actual goodness."[33] Although Jack is characteristically handsome, and symbolically linked to the Greek ideal Melville so often used for male beauty (he has, for instance, a "curly and classical head" [p. 237]), his physical appearance is not as important as his ethical role. He is characterized in the classical epic tradition by epithet—as "matchless Jack." He represents a kind of natural nobility among the men and maintains the aristocratic bearing of his fictional antecedents such as Jack Easy. Although he accepts the inevitability of "naval discipline" on board the ship, he is "a stickler for the Rights of Man and the liberties of the world" ashore (p. 17). His fundamental sense of the right and his willingness to challenge unjust authority—it is he who saves White-Jacket from a flogging—make him a representative of an innate sense of justice, a natural law that is far superior to the artificial codes on board the *Neversink*. His naturalness, and his masculinity, are signaled by his beard, which "amazingly" lengthens and flourishes when he deserts (p. 19) and which is ultimately removed by the power of the Captain in the "Massacre of the Beards." His "hard" exterior is combined with a soft heart and an "easy" manner (p. 14); his "natural" qualities are balanced by his skills at language and his familiarity with literature, above all Camões's *The Lusiad*, which he frequently quotes. Thus in his own way Jack too, although all masculine, is an androgynous figure, bringing together body and mind, nature and art. Still, even Jack cannot prevail in the world of a warship, and thus he becomes a figure of necessary accommodation to authority. Jack's appeal is thus potential rather than realized: it awaits its fulfillment through the crew, but they, in an early version of *Billy Budd*'s crew, ultimately prefer submission to rebellion.[34]

Jack is no sooner introduced than he is mourned, much as Harry is in *Redburn*. The near-elegy is briefer and less literary than the actual elegy of *Redburn*, but it is still surprising as a sudden reminder of the novel's retrospective narration and, perhaps more importantly, the narrator's own sense of loss. White-Jacket has just announced that "from the outset Jack and I were fast friends" when the power of this memory seems to provoke a farewell blessing, "Wherever you may be now rolling over the blue billows, dear Jack! take my best love along with you; and God bless you, wherever you go!" (p. 14). Although the friendship of Jack and White-Jacket is asserted, it is in fact rarely visible in the novel. Thus James Miller's view that there is a "progression of Melville's protagonist from the restrained but intense attraction toward Harry Bolton to an unreserved and total comradeship with Jack Chase" seems a bit wishful.[35] As usual, Melville does not seem to have known how to depict friends together (this remains a problem even in *Moby-Dick*, where Queequeg and Ishmael are married, but afterward spend practically no time together).

The role of Jack Chase is to act as an alternative to the three authority figures by suggesting a natural hero, one whose position of respect comes from inherent qualities rather than from rank or power. The men may obey the Captain or the master-at-arms, but they love Jack. Jack's role is not so much to offer personal friendship and affection to White-Jacket as to provide a means for the crew to recognize their own best democratic instincts and realize their potential for brotherhood. As an erotic figure, he suggests the way in which Melville habitually linked the appeal of the handsome dark figure to his ethical and political role; for Melville sexuality was a means that could lead to social harmony.

War is itself evil, and as an evil institution it corrupts those who participate in it. Even Captain Claret is not naturally evil but merely made so by "the usages of the Navy" (p. 367). *White-Jacket* is Melville's strongest statement against war and its destructive influence on all participants. War is, he declares, "a thing that smites common sense and Christianity in the face. . . . everything connected with it is utterly foolish, unchristian, barbarous, [and] brutal" (p. 315). Although the sea still retains its associations with freedom, warships constantly deny that freedom. When White-Jacket goes aloft, he feels united with the universe and calls out with joy for "the rover's life—the joy, the thrill, the whirl!" But then he adds that when he "speaks of the rover's life, he means not life in a man-of-war, which . . . stabs to the heart the soul of all free-and-easy honorable rovers" (p. 77). War is as opposed to the spirit of the imagination as it is to friendship. And yet we are to blame for it, Melville reminds us, for we accept orders, violate our principles, and engage in war: "the worst of our evils we blindly inflict upon ourselves . . . each man must be his own saviour" (pp. 399–400).

That insistence on personal responsibility, which accurately reflects Melville's view of human complicity, comes nonetheless in the epilogue that in many ways denies the thrust of the entire novel. It is hard to accept that the author of the rest of the book could accept this complacent waiting for God, the "Lord High Admiral," to redress the wrongs of the world. The epilogue seems offered more to suit the fears of his readers, no doubt a little concerned by the novel's revolutionary implications. For *White-Jacket*'s true conclusion comes, not in the epilogue, but in the final episode of the beards. While treated humorously, this episode is also a serious illustration of the possibilities of human interaction, even while recognizing that nothing can make the men prevail *within* the social structure of the military ship. Melville would apparently have to wait for "Bartleby" to explore the possibilities of passive resistance. It should perhaps be remembered that Captain, commodore, and officers, even with their scourges and threats, could not prevail against the united will of the men; all such authority rests, in the final analysis, on the consent of the oppressed.

After the first order to shave the heads and trim the beards, the men stand together, their beards rhetorically braided "together in token of brotherhood" (p. 357).[36] Soon, though, one man, under the influence of "habituation to discipline," gives in and all the men accept the authority and cut their beards, including Jack Chase, who "drooped" at this loss of his "manhood," forgiving the barber as the act is committed (a comic version of Billy's forgiveness in *Billy Budd*). However, even in their reduced state, after the failure of the mutiny, the men do find comradeship. Their ritual union is celebrated with tobacco, always a symbol in Melville of peace, contentment, and comradeship. The "community of pipes is a community of hearts," Melville asserts. As the ship approaches the shore the men go aloft, "and round our mast we circle, a brother-band, hand in hand, all spliced together" (p. 396). This is the final vision of the men, and it serves as an emblem of their union, at once sexual and political.[37] The brother-band forms a circle, sacred sign of unity that cannot be broken, and dances around the mast of phallic energy. In this transformed May-Day rite, the men take over from the traditional maidens, but the phallus at their center remains benign. The wars over, that energy is now freed from its role in aggression and killing and becomes an erotic center of human brotherhood. Only in *Moby-Dick* would Melville ever equal that vision of a triumphant future of manly love and a redeemed Eros. It is, of course, a millenial vision, as Melville suggests: the men now see the "long-sought" Promised Land, as Moses had from Pisgah. But the promise is there, and the means are at hand: it remains only to find the courage to love instead of hate, to dance where once the guns had brought only death. It is not a childish vision but a deadly serious opportunity to bring an end to the self-perpetuating and self-destructive acts of war and aggression.

Moby-Dick:
"Our Hearts' Honeymoon"

Moby-Dick is Melville's most extraordinary accomplishment, a single novel which alone would suffice to make him one of America's most important writers. Next to it, all the early works seem to grope toward a form, and all the later works to be haunted by the memory of that achievement. The accomplishment of *Moby-Dick* is to have found a way to transcend the conventional forms of nineteenth-century fiction, as if Melville recognized the extent to which those forms contained within themselves the ideologies that *Moby-Dick* needed to combat. No other work is so sustained by the connection between language and idea, by the recognition that language does not express content so much as embody it. The conflicts of *Moby-Dick* are the conflicts of pastoral and epic, of lyric and dramatic, as much as of freedom and fate, or any such abstract concerns. Characteristically, *Moby-Dick*'s resolution is hermaphroditic: the heterogeneity of the novel's final shape is Melville's attempt to create a form that encompasses forms, a "symphony" or "marriage" that brings together all opposites.

As I have already suggested, the novel itself, as bourgeois epic, is a fundamentally masculine, productive form. The lyric, feminine and nonproductive, offers a natural opposition to the directedness of the novel. *Moby-Dick* moves from form to form, never remaining long within a single genre. Its use of multiple voices is one of the characteristics that most makes it anticipate works of twentieth-century fiction, and like those more recent works *Moby-Dick* is also questioning the epistemology at the heart of the novelistic form. "The Doubloon" is indeed its symbolic center, or navel; and the coin produces as many responses as there are characters to observe it. Each speaks in his own voice, and Pip's voice becomes a commentary on it all: he can only conjugate the verb "to look," since perspective is all-determining. Ultimate knowledge is an illusion and a dangerous one at that; the search for ultimates leads the *Pequod* to its destruction. The rejection of the absolute does not imply a total relativism in *Moby-Dick*; it is the very isolation of the characters, cut off from certainty as they are, that makes the bonds of affection imperative. Pip's hopelessness is the mirror of Ahab's; it is the product of an isolation so total that all relationships become mere impediments. For Pip there remains only the fidelity of the slave.

Melville's most striking use of perspective lies in his creation of the narrator whom we are to call Ishmael. It is through his narration, and his own narrative, that we see Ahab. Thus even when Ahab steps on stage and speaks, he is a speaker in a dream (or nightmare) that can only be Ishmael's. Melville almost certainly borrowed the device from Shakespeare's *A Midsummer Night's Dream* or *The Tempest*. In Melville something of the same effect prevails: one can read the entire novel as Ishmael's dream, from the musings of Manhattan to the reawakening of the epilogue, a dream that is also a journey into the underworld of death. But the principal role of the Ishmael narration is to frame the story of Ahab. The frame narration is an essential part of the novel's structure, for it is that which prevents the novel from becoming the story of Ahab and his mad search; it is that which prevents Ahab from being the hero of the novel, although he is the protagonist of the quest within the novel. The frame narration is the equivalent of Rosencrantz and Guildenstern telling the story of *Hamlet*,[1] or, to remain closer to Melville's immediate sources, of one of Faust's assistants telling the story of *Faust*. The antiheroic nature of the novel is insured by its manner of presentation. It is in part a democratic poetics that determines this structure; for if there is to be a democratic epic it must be the story of an Ishmael, an ordinary seaman, and not that of a kingly captain. The two strands of the novel complement each other— Ishmael's journey of discovery and rebirth parallels and undercuts Ahab's anti-epic of defeat and death.[2]

The very structure of their respective journeys indicates the extent to which something much larger than personal conflict is at stake. Ahab's is an almost paradigmatic journey of purpose—whether one takes that purpose to be the hunt for the whale that inspires the ship's owners or the search for revenge that actually motivates Ahab. Ahab is part of the tradition of the secular quest romance, and the structure that corresponds to this tradition is linear and productive: it must conclude in the achievement of the goal, the making of the product, the bringing home of the bacon (or, in this case, the oil). Ishmael's, on the other hand, is a journey without an apparent goal. It comes about because of a sense of discontent and melancholy but it is not directed toward the achievement of anything. Its goal is experience itself, and Ishmael is a kind of picaresque hero, recounting his adventures. Unlike the picaresque hero, however, who substitutes an unending line for a teleological one, Ishmael replaces the line of the epic romance by the circle, by making return the ultimate conclusion. Other epic heroes have circular journeys, of course, such as Ulysses, but the interest in them resides almost exclusively in the nature of the heroic adventures along the way, and return itself is associated with particular values, domestic and sentimental. Ishmael never comes home, but he does break the line of aggressive intent, and so saves his life.

Ishmael is not an intrusive narrator; by and large he allows the story to tell itself. His digressive nature is an essential part of Melville's subversion of the novel's form and not as some have argued a sign of a lack of craft. It is part of the organic poetics of the novel, as Whitman's verboseness and apparent randomness are part of his organic poetics of the lyric and epic. Digression is opposed as a principle to order; it represents the disorder of the mind. A look at the careful organization of *Moby-Dick* makes it clear that Melville shaped the novel carefully but chose a shape that would do the least violence to the natural order of speech. The rambling manner is an important part of Melville's strategy of countering Ahab's epic quest, on both political and aesthetic grounds. The rhetoric of Ishmael *is* his character, as the rhetoric of Ahab's is his. This dual perspective has misled many readers, as Melville intended it to; since nothing intervenes during the Ahab chapters to remind us of the enormity of Ahab's sinfulness, we too may be caught up in that quest and (at least momentarily) believe in it as ours. Many readers of the novel have gone so far, indeed, as to see Ahab not only as the hero in the technical sense but even as the hero in a moral sense. The most astonishing example, of many, is that of C. N. Stavrou, who wrote, "Ahab alone is free. He alone is resolute and daring enough to gainsay Family, Duty, Hope, Fate, and Death." According to Stavrou, in Ahab's apostrophe to lightning, "there is that which bespeaks man's most sacred allegiance; allegiance to himself; allegiance to that integrity of being without which man is less than man."[3]

It is through the opposition of the two elements that Melville establishes his fundamental structure of the encounter between the two great myths of Western culture, the romance of the Golden Land, or the search for a lost Eden, and the quest for knowledge and power, or the legend of

Faust. In the earlier novels it is the romance of the Golden Land that is central. Perhaps because the fall of paradise had occurred in the South Seas before his arrival there, Melville's treatment of his journeys to the islands is always partially ironic: he seems to recognize the inevitability of loss even while continuing to perpetuate the dream of innocence. That dream is linked to the idea of a sexuality freed from concepts of guilt or ownership; hence for Melville the yearning for a recovery of the lost Edenic islands was linked to a search for a renewed concept of male friendship based on equality. Alongside the myth of innocence ran another potent cultural myth, that of the Faustian search for power through knowledge. For Melville it was the confrontation of these two myths that created the tragic situation of his novels. The heroes of the early novels are defeated by the power of the authority figures from whom they seek to escape. The radical vision of *Moby-Dick*, already prefigured in the friendships of *White-Jacket* and *Redburn*, arises from the way it plays off these two forces and from its demonstration that, no matter how seductive the figure of Faustian man, it is love alone, as manifested in the marriage of Ishmael and Queequeg, that can offer an alternative to the impending apocalypse of destructive, and ultimately self-destructive, fury.

The homosexual relationship is invested by Melville with radical social potential; it is through the affirmation of the values of nonaggressive male-bonded couples that the power of the patriarchy can be contested and even defeated. The homosexuality of *Moby-Dick* is thus in no sense merely the reflection of Melville's personal predispositions or merely the recognition of a reality of life in an all-male society such as a ship (in fact, it is crucial to note that the wedding of Queegueg and Ishmael takes place on land, in New Bedford, and that there are no scenes of intimacy on board the ship, which is exclusively the preserve of the values of the Captain) but is instead a construct deliberately employed as an alternative to the dominant social patterns inherent in the rule of the Captain. The destruction of the *Pequod* and its crew is a sign of the social disaster that for Melville followed upon the imposition of exclusive white male power in its search for control over all that is nature or nonself, while the survival of Ishmael is made possible only through the example, love, and self-sacrifice of Queequeg. Ishmael's return to the surface, and resumption of the narrative, is an indication, in one of the novel's symbolic patterns, of the emergence of the circle out of the straight line. It is also the restoration of the feminine and maternal to a world that has forsworn all softness and affection. Ishmael survives the cataclysm of patriarchal aggression to be restored to the lost maternal principle from which he has been exiled. This return is not a Freudian one, but rather a reassertion of the cultural values that the novel has repeatedly shown to be endangered and victimized by phallic power directed toward conquest. The circularity of the movement indicates its self-sufficiency. Whereas linear movement is always in need of the *other* to fulfill itself and is always bound up in time, circular movement is complete in itself and timeless. In Hart Crane's triumphant words at the end of "The Tunnel" when the river has finally been *re*crossed, "Here at the waters' edge the hands drop memory; / Shadowless in that abyss they unaccounting lie."

Ishmael's dual perspective as both protagonist (at least of the first part of the book) and narrator allows him to call attention to the possibility of succumbing to the claims of authority. The opening of chapter 41 is a sudden, and shocking, reminder that Ishmael has not been mere observer:

> I, Ishmael, was one of that crew; my shouts had gone up with the rest; my oath had been welded with theirs; and stronger I shouted, and more did I hammer and clinch my oath, because of the dread in my soul. A wild, mystical, sympathetical feeling was in me; Ahab's quenchless feud seemed mine. With greedy ears I learned the history of that murderous monster against whom I and all the others had taken our oaths of violence and revenge. [p. 155]

Ishmael is the human wanderer who is capable of acting for good or evil, capable of swearing love or death (indeed it should be noted that the oath of vengeance on the whale and fealty to Ahab is the mirror image to the marriage vows of Ishmael and Queequeg). His position in the midst of the action allows for his crucial choice between the poles of Queequeg and Ahab. And his complicity asserts Melville's view that total power is achieved through the suspension of human, fraternal responsibilities: Ahab may be a monomaniac, but it is the crew who make his journey possible.

The language of this passage is an illustration of the way Melville uses the power of rhetoric as a force for the suspension of self-control. It is precisely the enormous attractiveness (the seductiveness, even the sublime beauty of phallic power) of this extravagant language that renders it so dangerous. In these words Ishmael speaks the language of Ahab, the language of romantic power. His adoption of that rhetoric of excess is a sign of his temporary allegiance to the values of Ahab, the values of unbounded self. The images of "welding" and "hammering" hint at Ahab's Promethean character, while suggesting a fabricated unity that is destructive of the individual. Ishmael's "sympathetical" feeling here is thus far different from that suggested by the later image of the monkey rope as a figure of shared destiny without the suppression of identity, but it is nonetheless important to recognize the similarity of feelings that may lead to such different ends. Eros is a nondifferentiated force that can lead to the pastoral calm of Ishmael and Queequeg or the epic energy of Ahab and his men. The exuberance of the repeated adjectives ("wild, mystical, sympathetical") and the poeticism of the metaphor ("quenchless feud") signal the loss of awareness in sublime self-deluding ecstasy, while the sentence's conclusion, "seemed mine," alerts the reader to the fact of retrospective narration and the recovery from the madness that is inherent in the abusive use of language. If Melville delights in mocking the pedantry of the "sub-sub-librarian," the other extreme of language, rage without order, is seen as even more dangerous. Ishmael's "greedy ears" suggest a language that is consumed rather than comprehended.

In the end it is Ahab's language as much as anything that causes the destruction of the ship. For this language, with its insistent self-dramatization, with its preference for display over meaning, with its enforcement of subordination through a kind of hypnotic thrall, must eventually explode from within, or confront reality and be destroyed. Like a sentence rushing madly onward without any sense of itself, losing track of its origins and gaining speed even as it loses sense, Ahab's speech—and the speech of Ishmael that is like it—is language out of control, words that have taken on a power of their own. That language is sorely tempting; there is that within us, Melville suggests, that dreams of the glory of this high prose. But it is the prose of a civilization gone mad, of a culture that has lost all touch with nature and with the function of language as representation and communication. While no one would wish to return to the practically preverbal state of Queequeg—and his mock-Indian talk ("you gettee in") is designed not to reproduce his actual speech but to stand for his use of a speech at its most fundamental—that language is sufficient to establish a bond of love with Ishmael. As in all such questions, Melville takes the intermediate position, that of the "noble savage" or the Greek "middle way": a language with natural nobility, somewhere between the near-grunts of the preliterate and the verbal flights of Ahab. Ishmael's changing voices, his matter-of-factness offer at least the potential for the development of such a language.

Ishmael's narrative prior to the departure of the Pequod occupies the first twenty chapters of the novel, and it is during this crucial section that he meets Queequeg. The meeting of Queequeg and Ishmael lays the groundwork for Ishmael's survival of the catastrophe of the ship's destruction. Ishmael may not always remain faithful to the values expressed in these early chapters, but they remain there as a foundation to which he can return once he has freed himself of the lure of the Ahabian quest. The Ishmael of the first section is situated for the reader through Melville's use of two prototypes, the biblical Ishmael and the Greek Narcissus. The opposition between the two in fact suggests a shift from a biblical ethos to a Greek ethos, in ways not unlike those suggested in the following generation by Matthew Arnold[4] (Melville's interest in this central cultural opposition is confirmed by his return to it in *Billy Budd*). As the spiritual descendant of the biblical Ishmael, Melville's hero is a stepson and wanderer. His isolation from family and community leads him to a state of melancholia in which suicide seems the only option. Ishmael as prototype signals a brutal, vengeful biblical world of the fathers in which justice is vengeance and in which moralism and militarism unite to destroy beauty. Ishmael's response to his melancholic condition is to go to sea, for he feels a strong attraction to the world of water, which he links explicitly to the myth of Narcissus: "And still deeper the meaning of that story of Narcissus, who because he could not grasp the tormenting, mild image he saw in the fountain, plunged into it and was drowned. But that same image, we ourselves see in all rivers and oceans. It is the image of the ungraspable phantom of life; and this is the key to it all" (p. 14). As a figure of Ishmael, he is an image of human isolation, but as a figure of Narcissus, he is an image of the desire to overcome that isolation by joining self and other.

As a cultural figure, Narcissus has been taken negatively; he represents an exclusive love of self. For that reason the Narcissus reference in *Moby-Dick* has been taken as a confirmation of Ishmael's alleged immaturity, a sign that he is in some sense like Ahab, seeking to control the world and dying in the process. From this point of view Narcissus is what Ishmael *was*; but I want to suggest that Narcissus is what Ishmael *becomes*. It is possible to see Narcissus in terms very different from those that have dominated the cultural tradition, as Herbert Marcuse has shown.[5] Narcissus can be a figure of a generalized rather than a directed love; his search to embrace himself is then a token of the way in which physical pleasure and a sense of the body can replace the body-hating aggressive sexuality of possession. The suggestion at the very start of the novel that Narcissus is "the key to it all" indicates that Melville has undertaken a vast task of cultural revaluation in which the search to embrace the face in the water is no longer seen as antisocial. Melville's novel posits Narcissus as the representative of a contemplative force that can counteract the active force of industry and commerce epitomized in the whale hunt. Narcissus stands for a love that will not be harnessed to utility, that seeks instead a pleasure unto itself. The connection between the figure of Narcissus and the con-

cept of homosexuality is obvious; it is based not so much on the superficial identity of sex between the lover and the beloved as on the social
implications of a love that is self-sufficient. The gap between self and
other is overcome by a love in which other is revealed to be but the mirror
of self. In the legend, as given permanent form by Ovid, we know that
Narcissus dies for his love; but may not that death be seen as the social
expression of the fear with which such love is greeted, precisely because of
its subversive potential? In *Moby-Dick*, Melville joins the Narcissus myth
to his death-by-water theme, but he transforms its significance, since that
death is no longer seen as a fit punishment for the Narcissus figure, and
since it is in fact the role of homosexual love to offer a return out of the
water. The rebirth of Ishmael at the end of *Moby-Dick* is an assertion that
Narcissus need not die.

The impact of Ovid's *Metamorphoses* on Melville was clear in *White-
Jacket*.[6] That novel is structured around a transformation of the hero that
is simultaneously a rebirth. Significantly, the rebirth occurs after the fall or
"plunge" into the sea and is accompanied by a kind of surgery, a cutting of
the shroud that would otherwise drown White-Jacket. Important echoes
of this scene occur in *Moby-Dick*, including Queequeg's "delivery" of Tashtego and Pip's dives into the sea. But descent and rebirth are of greatest
meaning for Ishmael, who begins the novel by plunging into his own
unconscious and emerges at the end redeemed by the coffin of Queequeg.
Ishmael as Narcissus is a hero of a transformation myth, one who must
pass through death in order to achieve new life. There is of course an
element of parallel between Ishmael and Ahab, in that each of them gazes
into the water and finds a dark other self. But the differences between
these selves are enormous. Ahab's other self is Fedallah, a Mephistophe-
lean creature of demonic energy, while Ishmael's other self is Queequeg,
representative of all primitive and colonized cultures. When Ishmael joins
with Queequeg, he joins the sundered races of American (and Western)
history. Queequeg fulfills Ishmael's Narcissus identity by leading him to
the discovery of the body as a source of pleasure and instruction: Queequeg's tattooed body is a perfect emblem of his own Narcissus-like, self-
contained being.

As an image of self-love, Narcissus is clearly linked with the idea of
masturbation, and we have seen how important masturbation is for Melville both as a liberating act of self-discovery and as a social act, a denial of
the attempt to appropriate sexual energies for productivity. In *Moby-Dick*
as well masturbation plays an essential role by providing a way for Ishmael
to recognize the potential of pleasure as an element in social integration.
Masturbation is the alternative to the constant sexual thrusting of Ahab

and his quest; it is the manifestation of a quietist, passive spirit that can provide the vision necessary to survive in a world of mad energy. Ishmael is associated throughout the novel with scenes of gazing and meditation; although these always contain an element of danger (the danger of a self-absorption that denies reality), they are "one insular Tahiti." "The Mast-Head" is the chapter that most clearly explores meditation and reveals Melville's complex attitude to it. It is by mounting to the masthead that one can escape from the rigors of the ship and more particularly from the control of the Captain. At the same time the masthead is a figure of total isolation; the allusion to Simeon Stylites suggests that there may be a perfectionism involved in this desire to leave the world behind. Thus, although it is "delightful" to go aloft, it is also socially irresponsible. It appeals to Ishmael, the lonely figure we have met at the outset, but not to Queequeg who is always ready to "plunge" into life in order to acknowl-edge his place in the human community. The appeal of the masthead is the appeal of primitivism; it is the yearning to leave behind the complexities of an unsatisfactory world. Still it can provide the opportunity for friendly exchange that is out of place below; Ishmael and Queequeg can "lounge" in the rigging. And one cannot take totally seriously Ishmael's justification for vigilance among the men on the masthead: that they must be sure to see the whales or else betray their economic mission. Those jokes about the owners and their interests suggest that Melville is exploring the sub-versive nature of leisure here; lounging is uneconomic and dangerously self-indulgent. But what concerns him most is the danger of ignoring the reality of evil. As many readers have pointed out, Melville's treatment of the masthead dreamers involves a satirical treatment of the idealism of the Transcendentalists.[7] If to some extent *Moby-Dick* is an attempt to pose the question, What would happen to a Transcendentalist on a whaling ship?, Melville's concern is to show the dangerous inadequacy of a philosophy that denies man's darker nature. At the same time he is also concerned to explore the ways in which that idealism can be employed, mixed with realism, and made into the stuff of resistance. If the ascent of the masthead is a masturbatory fantasy that removes one from the social world below, it is a necessary step in the process of liberation. Inadequate in itself, it may nonetheless lead toward the discovery of the erotic and antisocial potential that will become the basis for the new self that may redescend. Ahab is, after all, the Transcendentalist, not Ishmael, and he lacks the ability to enjoy, that very power that can be explored on the masthead.

An excellent example of the seductive power of the masthead, and the social reality below it, occurs in chapter 61. Ishmael sways "in what seemed an enchanted air. No resolution could withstand it; in that dreamy

mood losing all consciousness, at last my soul went out of my body . . . "
(p. 241). In the instance, since the "resolution" Ishmael has made is his
oath to Ahab, it may seem a good thing that he can free himself of that.
But his freedom will do little good for a body without a soul. And in any
case his sense of freedom is an illusion: Ahab's quest goes on, even when
Ishmael is dreaming in the mast. A whale is spotted, and the crew leaps to
attention. The depiction of the whale suggests an analogy with Ishmael:
he is "lazily undulating," reminding Ishmael of "a portly burgher smoking
his pipe of a warm afternoon." But the whale's meditative state only makes
him a better target for the whale hunters. So too the portly burghers, in
their meditative indulgence, ignore the realities of the world beyond the
hearth. The killing of the whale is a sudden, shocking reminder of the
rapaciousness and cruelty inherent in the whale hunt. Because the whale
has seemed like a lazy burgher, his destruction is all the more horrifying.
Thus the warm, sensual atmosphere that opens the chapter is suddenly
transformed into the rushing energy of the hunt, and the whale is no
longer a "burgher" but a "monster." Even so, his blood "poured from all
sides . . . like brooks down a hill," the pastoral simile only serving to
heighten the horror by its very inappropriateness. The final death-agony
of the whale is a wonderfully powerful piece of writing that leaves the
reader almost ill with the sense of criminal waste and destruction:

> And now abating in his flurry, the whale once more rolled out
> into view; surging from side to side; spasmodically undulating
> and contracting his spout-hole, with sharp, cracking, agonized
> respirations. At last, gush after gush of clotted red gore, as if it
> had been the purple lees of red wine, shot into the frightened
> air; and falling back again, ran dripping down his motionless
> flanks into the sea. His heart had burst!
> "He's dead, Mr. Stubb," said Daggoo.
> "Yes; both pipes smoked out!" and withdrawing his own from
> his mouth, Stubb scattered the dead ashes over the water; and,
> for a moment, stood thoughtfully eyeing the vast corpse he had
> made. [p. 245]

Again the implied simile (gore like the lees of wine) adds to the horror of
the scene. And the mention of the pipe at the end recalls our initial sight
of the whale, and its comparison to the "portly burgher" with his pipe.
The pipe is regularly associated by Melville with tranquility and harmony;
it is both personally relaxing and also the occasion for social interchange.
The murder here of a pipe smoker by a pipe smoker thus accentuates the
sense of fratricide. Stubb's pipe is significantly dead, for he has lost the

ability to recognize the sense of fraternity between man and those he hunts. This killing, which is the reader's first introduction to the reality of whale hunting, is set up in sharp contrast to Ishmael's dreamy state on the mast. If he is to accomplish any change, he must come down from the mast. Otherwise he is in danger of ending like the whale, killed as he dreams.

Prior to his journey on the *Pequod*, Ishmael is a comic version of the hero, garrulous and opinionated. It is his meeting with Queequeg that changes him permanently. That encounter, presented in mock-romantic terms, is a recognition of the transformative potential of nonaggressive sexuality as manifested in male-bonding. When Ishmael and Queequeg pass their "wedding night" together, they pass beyond the taboos of conventional society in the manner of romantic lovers such as Tristan and Isolde and must face their own King Mark. In such myths the sense of social violation is strong; the lovers' union flies in the face of family or national hostility. But in Melville's treatment of the theme, rendered partially comic in line with the tone of the introductory scenes and also, probably, to defuse the potentially frightening aspects of this frankly astonishing scene of male marriage, it is necessary for Ishmael as well to overcome his own prejudices.[8] His ability to share a bed with a cannibal is proof of the power of affection to overcome the prejudices that have been accepted into our own attitudes. Queequeg's odd appearance, and Ishmael's comically exaggerated fears, distinguish this scene from the erotic dreams of *Typee*. It is perhaps too easy to fall in love with the one native who looks like a Greek statue; now Melville asks his hero to spend the night with a grotesque (from his cultural perspective) figure with no signs of Western beauty at all. Ishmael's ability to embrace Queequeg, and to overcome his own feelings of fear and disgust, show his worthiness to undertake the journey on the *Pequod*.

Ishmael and Queequeg occupy a very privileged space; they create their own world that is largely immune to the world outside. Although there are "shades and phantoms" at the windows, Ishmael finds himself "redeemed" by Queequeg, who can heal his "splintered heart and maddened hand" (p. 53). It is clear that it is Queequeg who prevents Ishmael from becoming another Ahab, from using his isolation as the occasion for a bitter search for revenge on the "wolfish world." Although the ecstasy that Queequeg can produce in Ishmael (he feels "a melting in me") is a loss of self, it locates that selflessness as a step toward reunion with a larger social self. For Western man is plagued by an overabundance of self, not an absence. Queequeg represents a spirit of community, one that serves instantly to begin a historic process of healing. He immediately takes out his money and shares it with Ishmael, in a sign that this marriage is to be one of equals, and that private property can have no place in such a world of sharing. Since the amount of money is specified as thirty dollars in silver, Melville indicates that Queequeg's act is the reversal of Judas's betrayal of Jesus. All of his acts make it clear that Queequeg is a "natural Christian," whatever his actual religious practices; in a world of false Christians, only the pagan can represent the values that Christianity had claimed to incarnate.

The act of social transgression involved in the union of Queequeg and Ishmael is also an act of liberation. By accepting the bed he shares with Queequeg, Ishmael faces the forbidden darkness of the unknown (represented in the novel by the story of crawling up the chimney the night of the summer solstice) and realizes that prejudice is based on a fear of the unknown. The several references to Sodom and Gomorrah in these early chapters (pp. 18, 46, 58) indicate that forbidden sexuality is an important part of that dark world. Ishmael's bond with Queequeg thus overcomes sexual and racial taboos by exploring the potential concealed within the world of taboo in which, as Freud suggested, the intensity of the taboo is directly related to the intensity of the desire. Ishmael's memory, prompted by his night with Queequeg, goes back to a childhood transgression, when he had tried to imitate the "little sweep" by "crawl[ing] up the chimney" and had been punished by his stepmother (or mother—it seems clear that she is the *step*mother insofar as she acts to punish and to deprive Ishmael of the maternal affection he expects). The story clearly indicates another sexual crime, linked to darkness and dirt at once real and metaphoric. Entering the dark man's bed, and perhaps even his body, recalls this primal crime—only to exorcise the fear through the realization that the night with Queequeg gives rise to no punishment. The only antagonism that remains—in those shocked to see men of different races together—is social. With Queequeg he can face down the prejudices of society and even remark with indignation, in his wonderfully comic voice, "as though a white man were anything more dignified than a whitewashed negro" (p. 74).

Ishmael the Presbyterian is joined to Queequeg the pagan, the New Englander to the South Sea Islander, the white to the dark, the head to the heart and body. Melville's comic mode of presentation must not divert us from the significance of these scenes; for they enact a transformation as complete as can be imagined in which all given values are revealed to be only relative and centered in a particular (Western) culture. They accomplish this change without the inequality that would have seemed almost inevitable had the terms of the union been heterosexual: Queequeg is no dark maiden trailing perfume. The marriage is thus at once a violation of cultural and racial expectations and a violation of sexual expectations. It goes beyond the homosexual images of Melville's earlier works, such as *Typee* or *Redburn*, which have significant pederastic elements in them, to create an image that is consciously egalitarian and in which sexual desire becomes a basis for social action.[9]

The marriage ceremony is sealed by smoking Queequeg's tomahawk pipe. This object is an important sign of the transformation that Queequeg himself makes possible; it is at once a weapon of war and an instrument of peace. The tomahawk's ability to be changed into a peace pipe indicates that things, like people, are not inherently good or evil, but rather contain a potential for both. Evil arises from the uses to which they are put. The tomahawk/pipe also reminds us of the multiple ways in which a single reality is perceived and thus is like the whale itself. The use of the tomahawk as signifier indicates Melville's desire to link Queequeg to the North American Indians; his union with Ishmael is in part the reconciliation of a historical divorce caused by white colonization of America. The Indian theme is crucial to *Moby-Dick*; we are surrounded by reminders that the American nation has caused the extermination of the Indian nations and that the kind of behavior that caused that extermination continues to prevail against new foes. Queequeg as a composite nonwhite figure illustrates the links between the destruction of the Indian, the enslavement of the black, and the colonization of all nonwhite peoples. Queequeg is a South Sea Islander, a Moslem (he celebrates Ramadan), and an African (he has a Congo idol). He is a representative of all darker races subjugated by Western belief in progress and civilization. By smoking the pipe with Queequeg Ishmael can reclaim his own lost heritage and restore the brotherhood of humanity. By its shape, and as an object capable of being either a weapon or a source of friendship, the tomahawk pipe is also allied to other phallic objects in Melville's work, most notably the hand organ of Carlo in *Redburn* or the lances and harpoons in *Moby-Dick*. The tomahawk lies between them on the bed, like the sword between Tristan and Isolde, but it soon becomes an object to be shared. Along with his black god Yojo, the tomahawk of Queequeg signals his role as the bearer of an Eros liberated from phallic aggression and thus free to engage in homosexual play. The tomahawk that is both pipe and weapon is equivalent to the phallus that can be either a source of pleasure or an aggressive instrument of power. The tomahawk is thus the novel's synecdochic presentation of the transformation that is at its center: the rediscovery and reappropriation of the phallic.

There are many examples of sexual word play in the novel, and it is worth observing that such play is itself an example of that transformation of values that the novel proposes. For the sexual jokes reveal a highly charged stratum below the surface of language used as conveyer of meaning—a level equivalent to the potential for sexual play beneath the surface of sexuality as reproduction. The emergence of the sexual pun is an example of a linguistic return of the repressed. In his well-known study of the phallic joke in *Moby-Dick*, Robert Shulman argued that "for Melville as for Ishmael the power of self is inseparable from sexual potency."[10] Such a view misunderstands Melville's subversive use of the sexual. Indeed it is necessary to rediscover a lost sexuality, one that is covered up by the hypocrisies of polite society, but it is also necessary to make that sexuality over. Like the exaggerated phallus of Greek comedy, the constant phallicism of *Moby-Dick* is a counterweight to its epic and tragic force and a reminder of its fundamentally comic structure: disorder operating ultimately to the restoration of an improved order. By removing the sexual from the area of the forbidden, by intruding his bawdy, Melville works toward a reinvigoration of a newly defined sexuality. The phallic jokes are always linked to power, not only the power of the phallus but the ways in which power employs the phallus. Thus Melville cites an "Irish author" on the "horn" presented to Elizabeth I by Leicester. Similarly, he wonders, with a wink, at the "allegorized meaning" (p. 384) lurking behind the presentation of the "tail" to the Queen. The queen with a tail (*queue* in French or *Schwanz* in German) is the queen with a phallus, an armed virgin as in his poem "After the Pleasure Party." Elizabeth I, the woman who ruled, is a perfect figure of the phallically empowered woman. Most importantly, he concludes his central phallic chapter, "The Cassock," with the joke, "what a candidate for an archbishoprick, what a lad for a Pope were this mincer!" (p. 351). (Some editions of *Moby-Dick* have censored Melville here, or believed they were correcting him, by eliminating that final "k.") The joke is anticlerical, of course, referring as it does both to the pope's use of castrati as singers and the use of "lads" as sexual partners for the ecclesiastical powers. And yet the mincer, or castrator, clad in his "cassock" or foreskin, wears the empty exterior of that which he has himself destroyed, as he continues the pagan worship of the phallus ostensibly destroyed in the biblical story of Queen Maachah; but it is the worship of an empty phallus. (Melville either did not understand or deliberately altered the actual method of castration from the removal of the testicles to the removal of the penis.) The true phallic idol is Queequeg's Yojo, and it is to that source of energy that Melville suggests Ishmael must return.

The most consistent, and important, of the many sexual word plays in the novel is the reference to the sperm whale. It is of course the "sperm," or whale oil, that provides the economic incentive for the chase, whatever Ahab's personal motives for hunting this particular whale. And the whaling industry produced an annual revenue of $7,000,000 in the 1840s, Melville reports. Is there any better example of the transformation of erotic energy into cash? Drawing on the ambiguity inherent in the language, Melville makes of Ishmael an agent for the recovery of that erotic potential. He does that not by abandoning the phallus but by transforming it from an element of aggression to a source of pleasure, thus repeating the motif of the tomahawk. The vision of Ishmael as he squeezes the sperm immediately precedes the chapter on the "minced" phallus, setting up a clear opposition between sperm as agent of joy (Yojo is a mirror image of O Joy!)[11] and the castrating energy of industry and church. The sperm-squeezing chapter is the height of the novel's imagination of a restored pastoral in which personal love and affection come to act as counterforces to the habits of aggression. In his reverie, Ishmael is no longer the isolated man but the perfect part of a unified world of sharing:

As I sat there at my ease, cross-legged on the deck; after the bitter exertion at the windlass; under a blue tranquil sky; the ship under indolent sail, and gliding so serenely along; as I bathed my hands among those soft, gentle globules of infiltrated tissues, woven almost within the hour; as they richly broke to my fingers, and discharged all their opulence, like fully ripe grapes their wine; as I snuffed up that uncontaminated aroma,— literally and truly, like the smell of spring violets; I declare to you, that for the time I lived as in a musky meadow; I forgot all about our horrible oath; in that inexpressible sperm, I washed my hands and my heart of it; I almost began to credit the old Paracelsan superstition that sperm is of rare virtue in allaying the heat of anger: while bathing in that bath, I felt divinely free from all ill-will, or petulance, or malice, of any sort whatsoever.

Squeeze! squeeze! squeeze! all the morning long; I squeezed that sperm until I myself almost melted into it; I squeezed that sperm until a strange sort of insanity came over me; and I found myself unwittingly squeezing my co-laborers' hands in it, mistaking their hands for the gentle globules. Such an abounding, affectionate, friendly, loving feeling did this avocation beget; that at last I was continually squeezing their hands, and looking up into their eyes sentimentally; as much as to say,—Oh! my dear fellow beings, why should we longer cherish any social acerbities, or know the slightest ill-humor or envy! Come; let us

squeeze hands all round; nay, let us all squeeze ourselves into
each other; let us squeeze ourselves universally into the very milk
and sperm of kindness. [pp. 348–49]

Leo Marx has written at length about the inadequacy of this scene, which
he links to the earlier scenes of solitary reverie. But like most critics who
have addressed the issue he mars his commentary by recourse to Freudian
judgments. The scene is "infantile," it represents "erotic fulfillment of a
childish kind," and, according to Marx, Ishmael will outgrow "his procliv-
ity to childish pleasure fantasies."[12] Nothing in the novel suggests that
Melville saw the sperm-squeezing scene as childish; indeed everything
suggests that he gave it an essential role in Ishmael's transformation. The
passage presents, in miniaturized form, the development that the novel as
a whole depicts. The initial scene is that of the individual with his private
masturbation; but that aroused eros acts to suppress, at least temporarily,
the forces of aggression. Unlike the masthead gazer who runs the risk of
falling into the sea, the solitary masturbator has the potential of freeing
himself from his darker self. Reaching a state of suspended consciousness,
the feeling of floating or melting, he then extends his sensuousness beyond the self and takes the hands of his fellow men. Solitary masturbation
thus becomes mutual, and group, masturbation, and there is an accompanying shift from the self to the community—a community erected by men
working, and playing, together. It may seem surprising to some readers
that Melville would locate a model for human harmony in a group of men
masturbating together, but our astonishment only reflects Melville's extraordinary imaginative and visionary power, equaled only in his time by
Whitman's similar depiction in section 11 of "Song of Myself" of the
bathers joined by their orgasms.[13] Melville's passage brings us from the
personal to the shared sexual and then to the human and social; it is his
most thorough exploration of the social potential of male homosexuality
to break down the forces of aggression identified with the patriarchal
structure. Men coming together are not men fighting each other, or even
men hunting whales.
    This principle helps to explain Melville's digressive style and the multi-
plicity of perspectives employed: as Roland Barthes has argued, "le sujet
accède à la jouissance par la cohabitation des langages, qui travaillent côte
à côte: le texte de plaisir, c'est Babel heureuse."[14] Melville's ludic style
amounts to a constantly reiterated assertion of the subversive potential of
play at the level of textuality. It operates to counteract the force of seriousness that is the verbal equivalent of production-orientation. So too Mel-

ville digresses, or appears to digress, as a way of offsetting the straightfor-
ward movement of narrative force. To digress is to chat, to interrupt, to
provide indeed an inter*lude*. For digression is, as Barthes has pointed out,
ill-absorbable by the "discours du savoir."[15] In this novel, in which *savoir*
is so profoundly questioned, the digressions serve to remind the reader of
the limitations of knowledge and its attempts to impose order on experience. For this very reason, the novel opens with its parodic versions of
scientific knowledge, those "extracts" which, like the etymology, appear to
provide meaning but instead offer only a confirmation of the relativity of
experience. The novel is thus inverted, or turned inside out, and the
"meaningful" divested of its power as the "playful" takes on a new creative
energy, a masturbatory poetics to replace the copulative poetics of narrative in the "discours du savoir."

   But this vision, the supreme realization by a Melvillean Hero of the
power of the Dark Stranger, now transformed from the personal encounter with Queequeg to the anonymous encounter with all men, cannot be
realized on board the *Pequod*, captained as it is by Ahab, the representative
of Western man's Faustian drive for power. The imagery associated with
him emphasizes his power, his isolation, his political authority, his antagonism to nature, and his aggressive phallicism. These qualities are, in fact,
aspects of a single identity, and their ascription to the Captain of a ship no
one can ever leave (it is striking that in the earlier novels the ships always
land at least once, thus providing the opportunity to escape by abandoning ship) indicates Melville's growing pessimism, even while he is giving
his most hopeful version of the male couple. The Captain of the *Pequod* is
the force that rules Western culture, and only a total revolution—sexual,
political, and cultural—can overturn him.

   The sequence of chapters from "A Squeeze of the Hand" through "The
Cassock" to "The Try-Works" effectively demonstrates the impossibility of
sustaining the vision of a harmonious world of mutual sexuality and identifies the obstacles. "The Cassock" is concerned with the ways in which a
patriarchal church has destroyed the innocent phallicism associated with
matriarchal rule (as Melville indicates by his reference to the destruction
of the idol, "longer than a Kentuckian is tall, nigh a foot in diameter,"
formed by the whale's penis and represented in the biblical story of the
destruction of the idol in the "secret groves" of Queen Maachah by her
son King Asa, a synecdochic narrative of the deposing of matriarchal
authority). The elimination of the phallic establishes an abstract authority
of putative fathers who must now act to control the dangerously subversive forces of a phallic, natural religion. The ceremony of circumcision (or
castration, for the two are connected here, as symbolically equal) is an act

of empowerment and deprivation. The mincer, ironically dressed in the very foreskin he serves to remove, is a reminder of the extent to which priestly garb serves to recall the priest's own castrated origins as servant of the mother-goddess. But the cassock has now become the vestment associated with the liturgical Christian churches, whose hypocrisy permits them to forbid the expression of any phallic power while at the same time enjoying, in their own "secret groves," the pleasures of boy-love. The pope and his lad are a reminder that Christianity has not eliminated the natural regenerative forces or the power of male sexuality but that it has transformed them from an agency of pleasure to a world of dark secrets and forbidden pleasures. Joy is made evil, by the ascribing of a single, reductive meaning to a natural force, just as Ahab transforms the whale from whale into agent of all blackness.

The removal of the whale's penis is merely one small part of the appropriation of the whale in the attempt to make it over into an object for human use, a means to man's ends rather than a being with its own integrity. The Church is one of the principal agents in the violation of nature, since it above all can only see energy as directed toward a theological scheme rather than valuable in its own right, but technology also contributes its share to the process of destruction. "The Try-Works" is a vision of an industrial hell, deliberately compared to a painting of the Last Judgment. The men at work here are almost totally blackened by the atmosphere, which seems to be of burning human flesh: the fire lights up the "tawny features, now all begrimed with smoke and sweat, their matted beards, and the contrasted barbaric brilliancy of their teeth" (p. 353). The Try-Works is the final stage in the destruction of the whale, the final assertion of man's ability to make nature over, to reduce it to what is usable, of which the extraordinary wastefulness of the whale hunt serves as a perfect emblem. Melville's astonishing accomplishment here is to have seen a link between the repression of sexuality, as seen in the interdiction of masturbation and the hatred of the phallus, the assertion of a false religious authority, and the triumph of industrial capitalism. For that capitalism, represented here by the infernal factory, depends upon the harnessing of the natural and its elimination as an independent force, just as productivity requires the suppression of the erotic (themes to which Melville would recur in "The Paradise of Bachelors and the Tartarus of Maids"). The fire imagery which characterizes Ahab links him to Prometheus, thief of fire, the Titan who would be a god.[16] He seems marked by lightning, and yet not felled. The very fire he seeks to free has destroyed his inner being, and he remains a hard shell, all male power without the capacity of enjoyment, an erection that can never come. Our first sight of him is striking: "His bone leg steadied in that hold; one arm elevated, and holding by a shroud; Captain Ahab stood erect, looking straight out beyond the ship's ever-pitching prow. There was an infinity of firmest fortitude, a determinate unsurrenderable wilfulness, in the fixed and fearless, forward dedication of that glance" (pp. 110–11). Ahab's firmness is a sign of his opposition to nature; while the boat pitches, he remains unmoved, so great is his imposition of the will upon experience.[17] The language itself embodies this contained, aggressive energy, in the explosive power of that astonishing series of alliterated f's. All his power seems concentrated in his eyes, which, in contrast to the sentimental glances up into the eyes of Ishmael while squeezing sperm, are always directed outward as agents of aggression. When he looks at the compass, his "glance shot like a javelin with the pointed intensity of his purpose" (p. 358); Ahab needs no quadrant since he has made himself into a compass, constantly pointed in a single direction, that of the will.

Ahab's links to Prometheus are appropriate, for Prometheus is the culture hero of a society that is strong, aggressive, and proud, that values technology (the power of fire to transform matter) over human relationships. Melville may grant Ahab his "humanities," but he sees that these are deeply scarred by the fires of desire. Although Ahab's language renders him attractive, in the manner of Shakespeare's villains, it also serves to indicate his moral inferiority. He is more machine than man, his humming seems "the mechanical humming of the wheels of his vitality" (p. 142), and his "private" crew is similarly mechanical, as if they were but the elements of his factory: "like five trip-hammers they rose and fell with regular strokes of strength, which periodically started the boat along the water like a horizontal burst boiler out of a Mississippi steamer" (p. 190). His famous soliloquy in chapter 37 illustrates his pride in terms that cannot fail to convince us of his final inhumanity: "The path to my fixed purpose is laid with iron rails, whereon my soul is grooved to run. Over unsounded gorges, through the rifled hearts of mountains, under torrents' beds, unerringly I rush!. Naught's an obstacle, naught's an angle to the iron way!" (p. 147). Stirring though it be, this is the language of territorial conquest and expansion. Seeing Ahab's soul as a railroad train may indeed convince us of his determination, but it must also convince us of Ahab's identification with the forces that built the railroad, conquering a continent and subduing nature. Ahab's speech illustrates the connection between the capitalist search for wealth and the patriarchal search for power; each represents an ultimate violation of the natural world that must in the end be avenged. The whale's destruction of the *Pequod* is a sign of the fate that awaits a society with so little regard for the nature from which it extracts its wealth or the oppressed upon whose services it depends.

Melville would later expand on the connections he first drew in characterizing Ahab when he wrote his mysterious tale "The Bell Tower" (published in 1855). There Bannadonna, whose name suggests his qualities as the exclusive male principle, banning women from his realm of power, is identified as an architect whose lust for accomplishment and power over nature leads him into a self-destructive madness. Bannadonna's *folie de la grandeur* is directly associated with sexual power: "To the sound of viols, the climax-stone slowly rose in air, and, amid the firing of ordnance, was laid by Bannadonna's hands upon the final course. Then mounting it, he stood erect, alone, with folded arms, gazing upon the white summits of blue inland Alps, and whiter crests of bluer Alps off-shore" (p. 209). Melville even borrows the conceit of Ahab's soliloquy for a description of the movements of the apparent robot in the bell tower, seen "sliding along a grooved way, like a railway" (p. 221). Although the tale is in some ways darker and certainly more grotesque, it is also closer to the allegorical tradition and lacks the dramatic power of the earlier work. The associations of slave labor and technological advance with sexual power and egotism are somewhat diminished by the science fiction trappings. Although the natural world triumphs, it is through the highly allegorical figure of Una (the figure of the first hour as well as an allusion to Spenser's personification of Truth); relationships have become exclusively those of power, and no alternative force is present (this is the case with almost all the works of the later 1850s). As in *Moby-Dick*, man's vain erections are eventually transmuted back into nature, reabsorbed by the very principle they have denied. The bell tower now seems the "black mossed stump of some immeasurable pine, fallen, in forgotten days" (p. 208), its high drama now lost to time and change, as the *Pequod* descends and leaves "the great shroud of the sea" (p. 469) to efface its memory.

The whale represents the natural world; hence the inability of critics to resolve their argument over its essentially good or evil quality. *It is.* How Melville would have appreciated the critical arguments: he who hated critics and saw such attempts as a foolish gesture at imposing order on existence. Ahab's desire to kill the whale is as hopeless (barring a final cataclysm, in which he or his followers destroy the entire world for the sake of "truth") as the sub-sub-librarian's attempt to list all the quotations referring to whales, or the cetologist's attempt to classify whales according to some principle of order (such as the librarian's ideal system of classifying everything by size!). Such a pursuit is akin to hunting a whale for its oil and never thinking about the physical whale that must die for the sake of the oil. The whale is whale before it is oil, as language is surface before it is meaning. Knowledge is experiential, not essential: "the only mode in which you can derive even a tolerable idea of his living contour, is by going a whaling yourself" (p. 228). As Tony Tanner has written, "If [*Moby-Dick*] has a moral, it is the very American one that we should respect the mysterious otherness of nature and not seek to possess it."[18] Language itself, Tanner reminds us, is a form of taking possession of things. Classification is the intellectual equivalent of whale hunting: it is the attempt to impose order, an attempt as destructive in its way as Ahab's murderous search. All systems falsify experience by denying its sensuousness and its malleability. This is not to say, of course, that one must then retreat into silence (Melville did after all write his novel), but it does suggest that one must approach one's subject with some sense of its integrity. In John Updike's wonderful metaphor, the artist or critic must "go to Nature disarmed of perspective and stretch myself like a large transparent canvas upon her in the hope that, my submission being perfect, the imprint of a beautiful and useful truth would be taken."[19] *Billy Budd* would return to this subject. There Billy's words and actions are repeatedly read or misread, from his arrival on the *Bellipotent* to his posthumous reflection in the various "accounts" of the events. His death, like the whale's, is a confirmation of a reality that must be processed rather than taken in its own terms. Like the whale he ends as a commodity.

Although the ship's owners and Ahab have separate purposes—"They were bent on profitable cruises, the profit to be counted down in dollars from the mint. He was intent on an audacious, immitigable, and supernatural revenge" (p. 162)—their interests are enough alike so that the owners entrust the ship to Ahab. Although they know him, they believe that they can make use of his single-mindedness as a means to their own increased profits. As James B. Hall suggested some time ago, in this "industrial saga" Ahab may be likened to the manager, placed in charge by the absentee owners, who, by virtue of a share-holding system, have no personal responsibility for the actions of the corporation.[20] Ahab turns out to be a disastrous manager, since there will be no (financial) profit from this journey, but Ahab-like men are made into industrial managers because their fearlessness and determination are essential parts of venture capitalism. Those who could stop him choose not to, out of the fear that they may lose their profits (the owners) or their pay (the men). Indeed, since the ship has a profit-sharing plan, the men are among the owners and thus have a financial incentive to press themselves ever harder. Ahab exploits the weakness he sees around him; he knows that the "romantic object" is not enough to inspire the crew for long—only cash can do that. "The permanent constitutional condition of the manufactured man, thought Ahab, is sordidness" (p. 184). Thus he uses money as a lure to the men, even while he knows that he dissembles his true purpose. That purpose the men must not know, for one alternative remains to them: mutiny, or strike. As always in Melville, that alternative remains hovering in the background, never fully realized.

Although Ahab as "supreme lord and dictator" (p. 109) of the *Pequod* is linked to the other captains we have examined in Melville's work, his portrayal is the most important, since it is the first to make explicit the connections between various kinds of authority. Capitalism is one major element in the chain; as we have seen, the profit motive makes Ahab's rule possible. In his depiction of Peleg and Bildad Melville reveals the religious hypocrisy that barely conceals the dominant financial motive. Bildad's comic farewell is an indication of the accommodation religion has made to profit: "Don't whale it too much a' Lord's days, men; but don't miss a fair chance either, that's rejecting Heaven's good gifts" (p. 56). As "fighting Quakers" (p. 71) these men are a violation of everything their religion stands for, notably nonviolence and social equality. But, as the communitarianism and pacifism of early Quakerism gave way to profits and war, so the entire religious and idealistic basis of the American nation retains only the superficial claim to moral conduct. By using the specific instance of the fallen Quakers, Melville implies a larger condemnation of a society that claims a religious faith it violates daily. As in the South Seas novels, Melville sees a Christianity that has lost all claim to moral authority.

The *Pequod* can be understood in many ways as the American nation— as we have seen, pursuing profit and power under the guise of morality. Alan Heimert has shown in considerable detail how Melville's terms are drawn from the contemporary political debate.[21] While some readers may doubt the details of his specific identifications (of Daniel Webster as Moby-Dick or John C. Calhoun as Ahab, for instance), he is absolutely convincing in his argument that a political parallel is intended. The "ship of state" is of course a familiar metaphor, and this one has thirty "isolatoes" rather precariously "federated along one keel" (p. 108). The quest for the whale is, at one level, at least, the pursuit of a "Manifest Destiny" that is bound to destroy the nation. For that policy rests upon an ethnocentric vision that presupposes the identity of progress and white American civilization. No wonder, then, that the *Pequod* is "a thing of trophies. A cannibal of a craft, tricking herself forth in the chased bones of her enemies" (p. 67). Calling the *Pequod* a cannibal is part of the same process of inversion that makes Queequeg the only "Christian" in the book, but it is also a direct allusion to the blood guilt at the center of American experience.[22] For the "Ethiopian emperor" to which the ship is compared is now an American slave, and the Indian tribe from which it obtains its name is now extinct. All three of the harpooners are nonwhite, as befits the laborers of the ship's microcosmic world. For the white man's mission requires the colored man's sweat: Ahab's secret crew are all yellow, like the Chinese who built "his" railroad. Slavery is shown as playing an important part in the system in "Stubb's Supper" where Stubb abuses and mocks the old black cook, who reveals at the end of the chapter his just-suppressed wish that Stubb be eaten by the sharks. Fleece may play the "darkey," but his thoughts are murderous. The possibility of a slave rebellion was a real one for many people of Melville's time, but fears of Indian vengeance (except in the West) were by and large past. Still, the name of Ahab's ship points to the nation's role in the extermination of a people, a process that was continuing during Melville's lifetime. It is no doubt by a kind of poetic justice that it is Tashtego, the Gay-Head Indian (another tribe now extinct), who nails the final flag to the *Pequod* as she sinks.[23]

The issue of slavery was important to all Americans of the mid-nineteenth century, but it took on special significance for Melville because of the role of his father-in-law, Judge Lemuel Shaw. Shaw's defense of segregated schooling, and his decision to return a fugitive slave to his master, made him part of the corrupt world Melville was attacking, although by indirection.[24] The chapter on "Fast Fish and Loose Fish" has particular significance in this regard. For here Melville turned to the language of the law to show the ways in which a legal system would operate to uphold the values of property as against those of individual liberty. His analysis shows the connections between the legal status of women, slaves, and colonies, linking them all by his fishing metaphor that underlines the symbolic nature of the *Pequod* and its hunt. The conclusion of the chapter is a hilarious parody of the judicial quibbling that ignores every significant issue, followed by a series of contrasts that illustrate Melville's tendency toward the multiplication of tropes. For all ownership may ultimately be considered under the canopy of fishing law. A woman who is married is harpooned, hence a fast-fish; if she is married again, she is re-harpooned and now "that subsequent gentleman's property" (p. 332). As women are the property of their husbands, so are conquered nations the property of the colonial powers, Ireland the fast-fish of Britain, or Texas the fast-fish of the United States (Melville's allusion to the conquest of Texas in the Mexican War). By these laws of property, we must imagine that a slave is a fast-fish, although if he escapes, should he not then be a loose-fish until chased down again? Melville's ironic questions are designed to bring forth the recognition that laws serve only to imprison men and that freedom is a rare achievement. By treating slaves and women as if they were property, that is, as if they were fish, Melville reveals the gap between codified law and morality.

The Captain's role as political leader of a morally compromised nation is sharply contrasted with the role of Queequeg, the chief's son from a distant island, who has come to the West to learn how to make his people "still happier" and "still better" (p. 57), not still richer or still more powerful. As the novel progresses, Queequeg plays an increasingly smaller part in the action and the symbolic structure, although he is still essential to Ishmael as the means of his salvation. Harrison Hayford has argued that the Queequeg of the introductory sections of the novel was a late addition to the novel's composition. This would explain why the Queequeg of the later sections seems so little individualized and would suggest that by the introduction of Queequeg in the opening scenes Melville sought to add a "reconciling principle" to offset the Romantic quest of Ahab.[25] If this is so, and Hayford's argument is very convincing, it would help to explain why many readers have failed to be convinced by the changes wrought in Ishmael by Queequeg. As Henry Nash Smith has put it, "the centrally important process is not adequately worked out in the novel."[26] It is asserted more than it is demonstrated, for one must keep in mind the Ishmael-Queequeg relationship throughout the entire novel, even though it is only alluded to occasionally once the ship has set sail. This neglect of Queequeg is the novel's only significant flaw, but it is one that comes close to destroying its effect. By allowing Ahab center stage for so long, Melville has fooled many readers into believing that Ahab is the hero of the novel or that, worse, there is no hero and the novel is a nihilistic statement of despair. It is obvious that Melville wrote *Moby-Dick* in haste and that he disliked revision. But it also seems likely that the relative absence of Queequeg from the latter part of the novel is related to Melville's inability—both personal and cultural—to situate his homosexual romance in a social context. Everything we know about Melville's biography makes us suspect that nothing in his life could have given him any clue how to present a sustained loving relationship between two men, and certainly no fictional models offered themselves. That Queequeg exists is a tribute to Melville's deepest desires for a love that would operate toward social reconciliation; that he vanishes is a heartbreaking testimony to Melville's inability to realize those desires.

However little Queequeg's role is worked out in the later narrative, it is structurally clear. The innocent Hero meets the Dark Stranger before embarking on board the *Pequod*. In part, the Stranger's disappearance from the action is justified by the transferral of his qualities to the Hero; it is because Ishmael has learned the lessons of Queequeg that he is able to function on the ship as an exponent of a restored sexuality and even to survive. A clear moral distinction is drawn between Queequeg and Ahab in terms of responsibility. Queequeg's brotherly love is not only sexual but social as well, transformed into action in two key episodes. He quickly jumps into the water to save the greenhorn who had just been jeering at the companionship between the two men of different races. The episode demonstrates his ability to love even those who malign him, and it is concluded by Ishamel's summary of Queequeg's thought, "It's a mutual joint-stock world, in all meridians. We cannibals must help these Christians" (p. 61). The comedy of the response—a comedy heightened by the surprising financial metaphor (itself an ironic response to Emerson) and by the inversion of expectations of the last sentence—only underlines Queequeg's commitment to recognition of human responsibility. Similarly, Queequeg's "delivery" of Tashtego when he has fallen into the "Tun" shows his prompt action on behalf of others; the rapidity of Tashtego's salvation contrasts sharply with the seemingly eternal abandonment of Pip. The obstetric metaphor underlines Queequeg's role as a giver of life. Queequeg's descents allow others to rise, from the greenhorn on the dock at New Bedford to the final emergence of Ishmael from the sea, buoyed up by Queequeg's coffin. Queequeg is the power of life-out-of-death, the true meaning of the story of Jonah, as opposed to the Calvinist reading given by Father Mapple. A male midwife, Queequeg helps others to be born, and that birth significantly takes place out of a vast tub of sperm. As he transcends the limits of gender, he unifies male and female and realizes the full potential of a creative force at once seminal and generative. Queequeg's "plunges" are dives into life. They clearly demonstrate the relationship between thought and action on his part, an integration of spirit and body that Melville contrasts to the idealism of the Platonist (read Transcendentalist), who is likely to drown in the sweetness of his own thought but who is unable to take action. Ahab's captaincy represents authority without such responsibility; Ahab is prepared to sacrifice the lives of all his crew for the sake of his own desires. He seeks explicitly to deny the community of human relations: "Cursed be that mortal inter-indebtedness which will not do away with ledgers. I would be free as air . . . " (p. 392). In fact, of course, he depends on many in very direct ways: on his cabin boy, Pip, on his nearly beloved Starbuck, on his Manilla men, and of course on the carpenter who must make the ivory leg on which he stands. His refusal to acknowledge such links cuts him off from the human com-

munity, and what might have been love becomes hate. His is no joint-
stock company but a hierarchical corporation; no democratic society but a
monarchical pyramid.

The political implications of Ahab's role are paralleled by the sexual
implications. As he had already done in "Fast Fish and Loose Fish," Melville acknowledges the relationship between political authority, property
rights, and the suppression of slaves or women. His discussion of the
"harpooned" wife makes it clear that he recognizes the political and sexual
metaphors associated with the harpoon. The chapter, "The Crotch," emphasizes the role of such aggressive phallic power as a violation of nature.
Opening with a reference to trees, the chapter sets in motion an image of
new growth, by branching, and establishes an organic metaphor that is
suggestive for an understanding of Melville's own digressive method. But
he then shifts abruptly to the crotches on shipboard that hold one end of
the harpoon, while the "other naked, barbed end slopingly projects" (p.
246). The crotch is well named, since it branches out into the cock, but
this cock, although naked, is barbed and mechanical. The harpoon crotch
is a splendid trope for the way in which the entire mission of the *Pequod*
(that colonizing, Indian-killing, nature-conquering mission) is a perversion of a natural organic phallicism into a grotesque mechanical parody
which cannot even come, but can only maim and possess. If the figure
associated with Queequeg is the tomahawk pipe, the figure associated
with Ahab is the lance (or the javelin, as mentioned earlier). Like the pipe,
the lance is an object of phallic dimension; but unlike the pipe, it can have
no positive, fraternal use. It is a language of pure meaning, cleared of
ambiguity and play. It is the sign of Ahab's role as patriarch and incarna-
tion of the Western rule of Logos. It is the sign of an aggressive heterosexuality linked to conquest and ownership. The inversion of the lances to
form goblets (a dark analogue to the inversion of the tomahawk to the
pipe) forms part of the ceremony of malediction against the whale. This
ceremony is not only a Black Mass, but a parody of sexual union. It
indicates the impossibility of fulfilling Ahab's Grail quest and restoring
the potency of this Fisher King.[27] The phallic power of Ahab and his men
is turned exclusively outward; it is a means of conquest. There are, then,
two kinds of phallicism present throughout the novel: a phallicism that is
largely divested of its sexual energy and redirected toward political ends,
the phallicism of Ahab and the phallicism of a perfunctory heterosexuality; and a polysemous phallicism that is not directed outward but that
retains a full sense of its own pleasurability, while it is at the same time
capable of extending itself into social action in terms of sharing. This
second phallicism is the phallicism of Queequeg, the phallicism of the

mutual masturbation of "A Squeeze of the Hand." Melville's biblical references[28] suggest that he recognized in many of the Old Testament stories
of the suppression of idolatry their origin in a conflict between a matriarchal religion in which the phallus was worshiped as a source of pleasure
and generation and a patriarchal religion that was supplanting the older
customs and replacing the benign phallus with the wrath of Jehovah. The
"Hebraic" qualities of *Moby-Dick* are signs of the novel's concern with that
imposition of male authority that lies at the heart of Western history.

Ahab is a "thunder-cloven old oak" (p. 111) that is unable to bloom
again; these hints at his impotence, like the suggestion of castration in his
loss of a leg, underline his loss of phallic potential. He is the "blighted
fruit tree" with a "cindered apple" (p. 444); in a striking reversal it is this
thoroughly heterosexual man who suffers the punishment of Sodom. His
inability to flower leaves him perpetually outside the world of pastoral
pleasures. He is, like his leg, perpetually stiff. His artificial leg is a marvelous synecdoche for his mechanical, contrived self and a perpetual phallic
energy that can never be relieved. He embodies the novel's epic element,
and the moments in which he is briefly tempted are cast as pastoral. But,
like Aeneas on his way to Rome, or Ulysses homeward bound, for Ahab
the feminine can only be a trap, a lure to draw man away from his higher
purpose. "The Symphony" is a wonderful vision of a harmonious universe in which masculine and feminine are reconciled; this divine androgyny is Ahab's last temptation, and he resists it to pursue the whale to
the end. Epic and pastoral—the conflict between them is as central to the
novel as the sexual or political conflicts. Pure pastoral may bring us to the
dreamy self-indulgence of "The Mast-Head"; pure epic will surely bring
us to the political insanity of the death-driving *Pequod*. Only Ishmael can
transcend these categories and so move beyond history to the redeemed
world of the epilogue in which nature has once more taken on a benign
aspect.

Ahab's element is fire, as Ishmael's is water; it is a fire that consumes
and destroys, himself as well as others. Fire is the active principle, water
the passive, and Ishmael must therefore move toward a union of the two.
This he finds in the novel's central figure of sperm, or hot water. With the
liquidity of water and the heat of fire, sperm brings together the generative power of fire with the calm of water. It is the final "creamy pool" that
restores Ishmael to life.

Ahab's end is balanced against the positive symbols of Ishmael and
Queequeg. Ahab casts his final lance, but the line catches him by the neck
and casts him overboard. He is destroyed by his own aggressive arm. The
rope that catches him indicates his bonds to the whale, the object of his

hate, and provides an analogous but reversed image to the monkey rope that joined Queequeg and Ishmael. The monkey rope is a sign of the human interdependence that arises from a recognition of fellow humanity; it acknowledges that "for better or for worse, we two, for the time, were wedded" (pp. 270–71). It has no top or bottom, for every responsibility is balanced by an equal possibility. Ahab's rope, on the other hand, joins self to world and is as linear as he is; it is a one-way rope that acknowledges only power. When Ahab perishes by his sword, it is Melville's acknowledgment of the vengeance that must finally be exercised by nature against its exploiters. For Ahab is, in effect, Logos as rapist, the culmination of a historical myth that values human knowledge and power over self-sufficiency and human affection.

It is Melville's extraordinary accomplishment in *Moby-Dick* not only to have identified this Faustian constant in our culture but to have begun the search for an alternate vision. Melville's work acknowledges, in a breathtaking way, the links between male aggression, patriarchy, linear progress, militarism, and capitalism. Against them all he sets the power of the male couple formed by Ishmael and Queequeg. He seems to have recognized in their union a radical potential for social reorganization, based on the principles of equality, affection, and respect for the other. Melville was surely not so naive as to believe that any homosexual union would achieve such goals. Indeed he seems to distinguish male friendships from shipboard buggery that merely recapitulates the power structure of compulsory heterosexuality. But he did see that, in the social context, the union of two men in a noncompetitive way might form the basis for a reexamination of man's relation to the world around him. As much as Whitman, and in a much more complex manner, Melville seems to have found a radical democratic potential in the male couple, one that, even in a world without women, came astonishingly close to realizing some important feminist goals. The marriage of Queequeg and Ishmael is a vision of a triumphant miscegenation that can overcome the racial and sexual structures of American society. The novel is indeed tragic from the perspective of Ahab, as many commentators have noted; but it is worth pointing out that it is also a pastoral vision of a restored harmony that might be achieved if only men would learn to love each other (individually and socially). With a full sense of the difficulty of achieving it, and the necessity of passing through the turmoil of life (Hart Crane's tunnel) in order to do so, Melville retained a belief in the power of the Golden Land, not a place but a state of mind, "not down in any map," which alone could have the power to restore life and set the forest blooming again. That Arden is first glimpsed in New *Bed*ford, and nothing can finally erase its memory.

~~~~~~~~~~~~~~~~~~~~~~~ **F O U R** ~~~~~~~~~~~~~~~~~

Losing Hope

The Dark Years

Moby Dick was Melville's last hopeful fiction, and even its hope seems abandoned partway through, only to be resumed, miraculously, in the epilogue. We can probably never know for certain the reasons that drove Melville ever further from the warm light that bathed his earliest books. *Redburn*, of course, anticipates some of the concerns of the later works for the horrors of urban reality, and its use of an antihero also seems to look forward to *Pierre* or *The Confidence-Man*. But Redburn himself survives, even if Harry is killed. There are few survivors in *Pierre* or *Billy Budd*. *Pierre*, like *Redburn* or *White-Jacket*, is partly about the fate of the artist in an unappreciative society, and its despair is greater because of its setting in "the world" rather than on shipboard. Melville obviously felt that his own work was unappreciated and misunderstood, that he was called upon to write in a manner that he found uncongenial and false to his deepest convictions. He wanted to tell the truth, ragged as it might be, not provide the symmetry of artistic falsification. In addition to his increasing cynicism about the fate of the artist in a commercial (and sentimental) society, Melville had, I believe, strong personal reasons for despair. For this extraordinarily lonely man, a man almost all of whose books depict the search for friendship, had in a short time found the friend he had yearned for and then lost him—a friend who was also considered America's greatest novelist, Nathaniel Hawthorne.

Hawthorne's betrayal of Melville occurred on several levels. It may well have been sexual, as Edwin Miller has suggested, largely arguing from the evidence of *Clarel*.[1] But *Clarel* can only be used to demonstrate Melville's desire for a sexual relationship with Hawthorne, not Hawthorne's response. All that one can say, with reasonable certainty, is that Melville believed that Hawthorne would refuse his desire for the physical expression of their friendship. He had reason, of course, to say that on the basis of Hawthorne's works, no matter what happened in private. But Melville must also have felt a strong sense of artistic betrayal. Melville had, after all, praised Hawthorne's strength and seen his "darkness." But Hawthorne was now writing *The Blithedale Romance*, a work that in addition to satirizing Melville himself in the person of Hollingsworth offered a weak, dreamy hero and an incredibly sentimental ending. It is a book that must have seemed to Melville to refuse all energy, political, social, and sexual. While Melville wrote of his Pierre who raged against the world, Hawthorne created the insipid Coverdale and killed off Zenobia, the reincarnation of his greatest creation, the Hester Prynne of *The Scarlet Letter*. To the literary disappointment must be added political disappointment. Hawthorne remained faithful to his old college friend Franklin Pierce at a time when Pierce had become a virtual apologist for concessions to the South and to slavery. Melville must have seen this apparent currying of favor with some disdain, especially since Hawthorne's behavior led to political rewards while Melville's family tried in vain to obtain similar favors for him. He can hardly have seen Hawthorne in the consul's office in Liverpool with total equanimity. And yet, despite it all, he loved Hawthorne, or at least the Hawthorne he believed he had once known.

Gentleness is punished in Hawthorne's early work. Clifford, in *The House of the Seven Gables*, is a clear indication of the price paid for gentleness in an aggressive, competitive world. The miniature by Malbone shows him as "a young man, in a silken dressing-gown" with a "countenance of reverie, with . . . full, tender lips, and beautiful eyes, that seem to indicate not so much capacity of thought, as gentle and voluptuous emotion."[2] This man of "exquisite taste" and devotion to beauty can have no place in the new, commercial world; his feminine values must give way to a more masculine striving. The death of the faun in *The Marble Faun* seems to reenact the same drama; it is not only a theological re-creation of the Fall but a sociological picture of a transition in cultural values and a psychological portrait of the eventual suppression of the androgynous faun. In "The Gentle Boy," Hawthorne gave an even more shocking portrayal of the fate of gentleness, and here he linked it to friendship. Ilbrahim, the gentle, outcast boy (whose name may anticipate Melville's Ishmael), is betrayed by his false friend. The scene in which Ilbrahim is lured by his friend, "come hither and take my hand," is one of the most horrible in all of Hawthorne's work, for the extended hand holds the staff with which he then beats Ilbrahim, and all the boys join in, almost killing him. The story is, I believe, a key to all the failures that run throughout Hawthorne's work, the failures, to use Forster's term, to "connect." These failures derive out of fear—fear and the experience of betrayal. Hawthorne's gentle, delicate boys and men have dared to love and have been punished for it. As a consequence, they withdraw and refuse all love, for love may be dangerous. This sense of refusal is nowhere expressed more fully than in the words of Kenyon in *The Marble Faun*, in a speech that seems to arise not from the necessity of the narrative so much as from some inner necessity on the part of the author. It is, I think, a version of Hawthorne's answer to Melville. Kenyon refuses the possibility of helping or loving Donatello, for he says: ". . . I am a man, and, between man and man, there is always an insuperable gulf. They can never quite grasp each other's hands; and therefore man never derives any intimate help, any heart-sustenance, from his brother man, but from woman—his mother, his sister, or his wife."[3] Men fail to help each other; they fail to love; only women remain.

Melville's sense of loss underlies all of his work of the 1850s, after *Moby-Dick*. Literary failure, the decline of the nation and the impending war, and personal isolation combined to deepen his sense of hopelessness. And yet he clung to memory, for increasingly it was only memory that could sustain him. He relived his friendship with Hawthorne in several crucial poems that testify to the importance of that relationship and to Melville's sense of loss. "Monody" is the poem Melville wrote at the time of Hawthorne's death, and it is a magnificent testament both to the force of Melville's love and the sense of permanent impossibility that followed upon their "estrangement":

> To have known him, to have loved him
>   After loneness long;
> And then to be estranged in life,
>   And neither in the wrong;
> And now for death to set his seal—
>   Ease me, a little ease, my song!
>
> By wintry hills his hermit-mound
>   The sheeted snow-drifts drape,
> And houseless there the snow-bird flits
>   Beneath the fir-trees' crape;
> Glazed now with ice the cloistral vine
>   That hid the shyest grape.

The image of the last two lines, "the cloistral vine / That hid the shyest grape," is an important reason for associating Hawthorne with the character Vine in *Clarel*, where the "cloister" is also an important metaphor. Personal isolation, represented here by the monastic (or conventual) image of the "cloister," is linked to death and the loss of sexuality. For the "shyest grape" is surely a sexual reference to the hidden penis (or genitals generally)[4] that Melville longed to see and to taste and that, now with Hawthorne's death, he knew he would never see. The Vine of *Clarel* is a man who lives by control of self, by curb of flesh, by mortification of desire: "Like to the nunnery's denizen / His virgin soul communed with men / But through the wicket." The convent can be the only place for those who would preserve their virginity (spiritual or physical) at any price—and what price they pay in human relations! Melville added, asking rhetorically about the source of this withdrawal on the part of Hawthorne/Vine, "Was it clear / His coyness bordered not on fear— / Fear or an apprehensive sense?" (part 1, canto 29). *Clarel*, written out of Melville's breakdown, is Melville's attempt to rouse himself from the despair into which he had fallen. To do that, he had to come to terms with Hawthorne. And that meant acknowledging the impossibility of ever fulfilling his desires, of ever finding a male friend who could join beauty and intelligence, the grace of nature with the wisdom of art.

Clarel first sees Vine in a way that emphasizes his links to Hawthorne: "As were Venetian slats between, / He espied him through a leafy screen" (part 2, canto 27). Vine is thus hidden by a veil or covering (indeed a vine concealing a grape), which can hardly fail to remind us of Coverdale's Hermitage in *The Blithedale Romance* or of many of the other disguises, masks, and concealments with which Hawthorne was so concerned (and of course there is a wonderful element of revenge if Melville recognized himself in the character of Hollingsworth: now he turns the tables on Hawthorne/Coverdale/Vine and spies on him).[5] At the same time, this figure between slats or blinds recalls the dangerous siren eyes of Melville's "In a Bye-Canal." Clarel then joins Vine, who seems to warn him, "Ah, tarry, for at hand's a sea / Whence ye shall never issue out / Once in." That dangerous sea is, especially in the context of *Moby-Dick*, clearly the sea of self, or the unconscious. Clarel has been warned, and Vine seems to offer him not a turbulent sea but a calm lake:

> Pure as the rain
> Which diamondeth with lucid grain,
> The white swan in the April hours
> Floating between two sunny showers

> Upon the lake, while buds unroll;
> So pure, so virginal in shrine
> Of true unworldliness looked Vine.

But his very purity, expressed through the images of the swan, the bud (strangely anticipating *Billy Budd*), and the nun, arouses desire in Clarel. Clarel yearns for a union of souls, an affirmation of brotherhood:

> How pleasant
> In another such sallies, or in thee, if said
> After confidings that should wed
> Our souls in one:—Ah, call me *brother*!

The mystical marriage, like that of Queequeg and Ishmael, should create a true spiritual bond. But Vine does not respond, and Clarel wonders if he thinks (perhaps borrowing from Kenyon's response to Donatello):

> But for thy fonder dream of love
> In man toward man—the soul's caress—
> The negatives of flesh should prove
> Analogies of non-cordialness
> In spirit.

Out of a presumed physical impossibility comes a spiritual refusal; because there can be no physical relationship, there can be no spiritual one. In these lines we see Melville's clear links between the sexual and the emotional; by denying the sexual, the emotional is also denied, lest the line between friendship and sexual love be crossed.

Melville treated the subject of a refused sexuality in one last poem, "After the Pleasure Party," an astonishing work for its time (the exact date of composition is unknown; I am treating it here as written after *Clarel*, but my argument does not depend on that supposition). The poem is concerned primarily with the realization of the division into two sexes and the yearning for a rediscovery of an androgynous self. It is also a defense of the single life, and, I suspect, in these terms an answer to Vine/Hawthorne's assumption that there can be no real physical relationship between men, hence no real spiritual relationship. There can be none, of course, as long as one imagines oneself in terms of a single, characteristic organ—that is, male, with penis, female, with vagina. If, however, one can imagine oneself, as Melville does in "After the Pleasure Party," as bisexual, with both penis and vagina, or, in male homosexual terms both so-called active and passive, then one can be both giver and receiver, male and female in one. This is, the poem suggests, man's original condition and the state to which s/he yearns to return. Urania, the Muse of the poem, is of course the muse of astronomy, hence a figure of the learned woman, or armed virgin, and a recollection of Plato's Aphrodite Urania, the goddess of a spiritualized homosexual love.[6] The poem celebrates the armed virgin, the goddess with a penis, the body with a brain, as a symbol of a reunified sensibility in which the divisions between male and female have been reconciled in a triumphant androgyny. In this context, Melville turns to his Hawthorne image:

> When after lunch and sallies gay
> Like the Decameron fold we lay
> In sylvan groups; and I—let be!
> O, dreams he, can he dream that one
> Because not roseate feels no sun?
> The plain lone bramble thrills with Spring
> As much as vines that grapes shall bring.
> [ll. 66–72]

Although Melville uses a female persona, the first part of the stanza clearly recalls the sylvan grouping of *Clarel* (which in turn may recall Melville's famous picnic in the Berkshires with Hawthorne), even echoing the term "sallies," and the Decameron reference hints at sexual adventures. But the story is abruptly cut off; "let be" seems to indicate the speaker's (and Melville's) desire not to relive this painful experience. Because I am childless and "plain," she wonders, does he imagine that I am without sexual response? "Roseate" conceals a particular reference to Hawthorne as father, especially in the context of the vine/grape image of the final line quoted. Not only are roses a general sign of natural fertility and passion, but one of Hawthorne's daughters was named Rose. In the speaker's reference, one not "roseate," one childless, is not necessarily sun-less. By extension, relationships that are nonproductive (sterile in a conventional or technical sense) can be as thrilling, as joyful, and as renewing as those that give birth (yield fruit). Whatever "Vine" may have thought, it is clear that for Melville a homosexual relationship can be the source of new life.

"After the Pleasure Party" is not only a defense of homosexuality but a warning against the consequences of repression. The poem itself is preceded by a six-line epigraph, termed "lines traced under an image of Amor threatening," which warns of Amor's revenge if he is too long "slighted": he will bring "Tempest even in reason's seat." The speaker of the poem believes that she, as an intellectual, is exempt from love, but even after "pale years of cloistral life," it comes again. In a wonderful image, she recognizes the force of sexual energy within the self:

soon or late, if faded e'en
One's sex asserts itself. Desire,
The dear desire through love to sway,
Is like the Geysers that aspire—
Through cold obstruction win their fervid way.
[ll. 28–32]

As a geyser breaks through the surface of the earth, so sexual desire finally erupts even after the most valiant attempts to suppress it. The human, intellectual desire to assert superiority over Amor is like the attempt to deny Nature—and equally doomed to failure. What happens to those who realize this too late?

Melville's last poems are devoted to reminiscence and nostalgia, even while his philosophical views grew darker. He remembered fondly his sailor companions in a number of poems. In "John Marr," for instance, he was able to conjure up the past and restore that paradise lost so long ago:

I yearn as ye. But rafts that strain,
Parted, shall they lock again?
Twined we were, entwined, then riven,
Ever to new embracements driven,
Shifting gulf-weed of the main!
And how if one here shift no more,
Lodged by the flinging surf ashore?

Nor less, as now, in eve's decline,
Your shadowy fellowship is mine.
Ye float around me, form and feature:—
Tattooings, ear-rings, love-locks curled;
Barbarians of man's simpler nature,
Unworldly servers of the world.
Yea, present all, and dear to me,
Though shades, or scouring China's sea.
[pp. 166–67]

The barbarians of *Typee* and *Omoo* are joined to the sailor-lovers of the other works and look forward to that final "barbarian," Billy Budd. Sailors are as out of place on land as barbarians are in civilized society. Though serving the world, they remain "unworldly." W. H. Auden commented that "the sailor on shore is not bound by the law of the land and can therefore do anything without guilt";[7] he attributed the homosexual attraction to sailors to this fact. Certainly a large part of the appeal of the sailor is his quality as rover, or omoo. As a free spirit, he seems immune to

the frustrations of life within society, even though he is subject to a perhaps greater tyranny on board the ship. Such lines as these demonstrate
the continuing efficacy of the myth of the loss of Eden for Melville and its
specifically sexual connotations: "Twined we were, entwined, then riven."
But that paradise can only exist in memory. If the earlier works still enter-
tain some hope of recovering the lost past, or of discovering access to it
through friendship, that hope is no longer present in these poems, or in
Billy Budd.

Melville's growing darkness was determined not only by a sense of
personal loss. Political and social events of the 1850s and later, leading to
the Civil War and the subsequent emergence of a new northern industrial
capitalist society, were a source of deepening pessimism. Human affection
no longer seemed capable of exerting any real force in human affairs.
Slavery continued to be the most offensive stain on the national fabric, but
northern emancipators were often blinded by their own self-righteous
ignorance and by a commitment to a new industrial slavery that ap-
proached actual bondage in its horrors. The works of the 1850s, after
Moby-Dick, are almost obsessively concerned with various ways in which
friendship is betrayed. The human relationships in the stories of this period are parodies of the loving relationships of the earlier works: they are
relationships of power, as in "Benito Cereno" 's exploration of the master/
slave relationship, or in "Bartleby, the Scrivener" 's exploration of the
employer/employee relationship. Melville's view of the Church in these
years centered on its violation of its apparent commitment to brotherly
love and its corresponding transformation into a social institution based
on wealth, as in "The Two Temples." Friendship itself seems to have been
appropriated and made over into a dangerous, even malevolent force. The
assertion of friendship is but another of the confidence games played in
The Confidence-Man, where over and over again professions of friendship
turn out to be false, frequently means for selfish purposes and financial
advantage. Orchis's betrayal of his friend China Aster is representative of
the pattern of duplicity that operates through the guise of friendship. It is
as if, from the time of *Moby-Dick* on, Melville was unable to portray the
relationship between two men without raising the possibility of exploitation and disappointment. Looking beneath the surface, he finds only
power and frustrated lust. Even "the man with the weed" (in *The Confidence-Man*), who seems at first to be able to throw "off in private the cold
garb of decorum, and so giv[e] warmly loose to his genuine heart," is not
only a foolish optimist like all the Transcendentalists in the novel but also
another false figure in disguise. His commentary on Tacitus, strikingly
delivered by one so untaciturn, leads in the end to an attempted seduction

of the "young gentleman with a swan-neck, wearing a lady-like open shirt collar." Both are false, the man with the weed because he conceals his desire in sententious rhetoric, and the young gentleman because his costume suggests an androgyny that he is apparently unwilling to acknowledge. Although "fascinated" with the man with the weed, he "abruptly retire[s]" as soon as the other pointedly suggests that he "have confidence in *me*" (p. 27). In *Pierre*, the novel published only a year after *Moby-Dick*, Melville attempted to locate his explorations of sexual politics within the confines of the domestic novel. While such a strategy could easily reveal the absurdities of the genre, it prevented Melville from exploring the subversive nature of friendship as he had in the earlier novels. Here that subversive role is taken over by a real or metaphoric incest, in which Pierre both rebels against and embraces the dead father by marrying his putative dark half-sister. This forbidden love, at once deeply sensual and absolutely pure, may represent the displacement of a homosexuality perceived with ambivalence. Pierre's decision to embrace Isabel means not only the rupture of his engagement to Lucy but also the loss of his friendship with Glen Stanley. The two cousins have known "the empyrean of a love which only comes short, by one degree, of the sweetest sentiment entertained between the sexes" (p. 216). Melville's repeated references to the two kinds of love—to, for instance, "those who love beneath the cestus of Venus" or the "Aphroditean devotees"—suggest that although he claims to see "love-friendship of boys" as a preliminary stage of development preceding mature heterosexual love, he also imagines it as an alternate expression of love, only suppressed "in many cases." The framework of the domestic novel provided no opportunity for the exploration of the Glen/Pierre relationship, and much of its energy seems therefore to have been transferred to the theme of betrayal and double love in the triangle Pierre/Lucy/Isabel, with Glen as avenging spirit of family and propriety.

The novel is based on material that seems still undigested, but much of its torment comes from the attempt to distinguish between a pure spiritual love and an impure physical love. With all the qualities of dark lover passed on to Isabel, Pierre's relationship with her bears the potential of offering a counterforce to the world of domestic sentiment and family obligation like that invested in Marnoo or Queequeg. But Pierre is unable to bring love and lust together, as his quotation of Shakespeare's Sonnet 144 in the last pages of the novel suggests ("Away!—Good Angel and Bad Angel both!—For Pierre is neuter now!"). In the context of the sonnets, of course, the opposition is between the fair young man and the dark lady, and the allusion here may well indicate the displacement of the boy-love theme onto the pure maiden. The form will not permit such radical energies, however, and Pierre dies mad, betrayed by the world he has attempted to purify. Renouncing the body, and attempting to expiate his father's sexual guilt, he finds himself embracing the body and confronting the "dark" sexuality of incest and/or adult homosexuality. In the form Melville has chosen there seems no way out but for him to die.

The Dark Lady/Fair Maiden dichotomy is one that is widely employed in the literature of the nineteenth century, of course, but it is one that is likely to become confused when it is complicated by the additional issue of homosexuality. For homosexuality is simultaneously perceived as dark and fair. It is fair insofar as it represents the idea of moral purity and innocence and as it is associated with spiritual love, ideas that were emphasized in discussions of homosexuality in the later nineteenth century. But it is also dark, insofar as it represents a forbidden love, one that may be said to explore the underground of consciousness. It is certainly "dark" when judged from the perspective of society, and hence it is naturally linked to other forms of social transgression, like incest, as part of the Romantic beauty of evil, chronicled so effectively by Mario Praz. Seeing this fundamental ambiguity drawn from the cultural context enables us to place *Pierre* at the heart of Melville's work, from the attraction/revulsion of *Typee* that suggests simultaneous sexual desire and fear to *Billy Budd*'s joining of the Dark Stranger with the Fair Maiden in the figure of Billy. The progression, and particularly the decline after the portrayal of Queequeg, suggests an increasing attempt to control the very sexuality that exerted such a strong appeal. Never again could Melville celebrate the power of a released sexuality to transform man's nature. In Melville's last fiction the Captain would at last prevail, although in deeply flawed ways that leave Melville's heart still with Billy.

"Benito Cereno" and "Bartleby, the Scrivener" are both studies in the relationship between a "good" man and an evil world and thus have direct relevance to Melville's later characterization of Captain Vere. All three works deal with the problem of complicity.

Like *Billy Budd*, "Benito Cereno" is a study in perception, most of the story narrated through the inadequate eyes and tongue of Captain Amaso Delano. The American captain eventually learns the "facts" of the slave mutiny, but his own subtle racism colors all his perceptions. He seems to believe that "justice" can be done in the colonial court, without ever recognizing the enormous gap between a natural justice that would preclude the taking of slaves and a political justice that is based on property rights. If one can be horrified at the thought of the violence practiced by Babo and the rebels, one must be equally horrified at a system that has allowed these blacks to be captured and shipped into servitude as if they

were animals (indeed one of the supreme ironies occurs in Delano's perception of the black mother and child as a doe with her fawn: his trope for
her must be bestial even if benign). Both "Benito Cereno" and *Billy Budd*
are set during the French Revolution (1799 and 1797, respectively) as if
to emphasize their political themes and the relationship between the various forms of tyranny.

The lawyer-narrator of "Bartleby, the Scrivener" is another blind observer who is too convinced of his own generosity to see the evil and
inhumanity of the system in which he participates. His situation illustrates
the sterility of a law divorced from morality. His dilemma is that of the
"good boss" whose integrity is inevitably compromised. He is a jailer who
can never understand that even good treatment of a prisoner cannot allevi-
ate the fundamental fact of imprisonment. Bartleby can only assert his
humanity by "declining," by a passive resistance that is an assertion of an
underlying free self that lacks the ability to rebel. Bartleby the wage slave
of meaningless work can only triumph by destroying himself.

Both the lawyer and Bartleby are bachelors, a state that Melville uses to
suggest the removal of the individual from the world of social relationships, from Ahab's "inter-indebtedness." As bachelors, they inhabit a sterile world in which work leads to no creativity. This idea was central to
Melville during this period and would recur later in the account of the
speaker in "After the Pleasure Party" as well as in the bachelor Vere. It is
more fully explored in the paired narrative, "The Paradise of Bachelors
and The Tartarus of Maids." This is one of several such paired stories from
this period, as if Melville had found in the form a way to express a sense of
irreconcilable opposites. The bachelors, in the story devoted to them, are
seriously debased versions of their Templar ancestors. From the homosexuality of the actual Templars (according to the accusations, at least), they
have subsided into a complacent celebration of privilege through eating
and drinking, inhabiting their "snug cells" (p. 232) of self-centeredness.
Their meal is a parody of Plato's *Symposium* (the waiter is jokingly called
Socrates), since any sense of ascending love has been lost. Homosexual
love, with its potential for the realization of divine beauty, has been transformed into homosocial "fraternity" with its implicit misogyny and its
sublimation of eros into physical excess. The "bachelors" of this world no
longer partake either of the ritual homosexuality of the Templars or of the
philosophically based homosexual love of Greece; they are instead a sign
of the debased ways in which alone those sentiments can be expressed in
mid-nineteenth-century England.

By pairing this story with that of the maids, Melville makes it clear that
his purposes extend beyond providing a critique of the comfortable bach-

elors in their pleasures of the table. Their privilege is purchased by the labor of the maids who work in the factory. That factory is the inverted image of the paradise of bachelors, as poverty is the inverted image of wealth, or female oppression that of male power. The hellish factory is presided over by a bachelor, so that the erotic transformation that underlies the tale is made explicit; female sexuality is employed to produce a commodity, the sale of which provides profit for the male owners. The women factory workers, drawn in part from a realistic social landscape of New England or the north of England, serve to represent the larger process by which the erotic is harnessed to the needs of production, and nature made to serve man. Thus "The Tartarus of Maids" continues the brilliant analysis of *Moby-Dick*, in which Melville first traces the connections between a series of dualisms, nature/society, female/male, black/white, body/mind, and so forth. In the shorter compass of this work, the analysis becomes even more pointed: the aggression of the "bachelors" is emphasized by the bloody imagery of the second section, effectively pointing up the ways in which those elegant men's club meals are provided.

The sterility of the men, associated with their status as "bachelors," comes thus not from the fact that they are not married but from the fact that they have suppressed the erotic. Melville's goal remains a rediscovery and reappropriation of the erotic, such as that indicated in the masturbatory visions of Ishmael. The factory is a perfect trope for the way in which a principle of dissemination, of the dispersion of life force, can be corrupted into one of directed energy and production. The factory system not only uses real women and destroys them for the sake of profit, but it also represents an attitude that places no value on things in themselves and sees them only as means. This is the fundamental error of a capital/labor relationship, as it is that of the male/female relationship in conventional nineteenth-century society. De-eroticizing their homosexual selves, the bachelors simultaneously lose the possibility of establishing a relationship with women on a basis of equality. Only when sexuality is restored to a place of free play and spiritual growth, the story suggests in terms borrowed from the *Symposium*, can it be freed from the concept of use. Thus the story's link of female labor and gestation; as long as women are thought of as a means for men to conceive children (or make profit) they cannot be seen as ends in themselves.

Delano, the lawyer, and Captain Vere all believe in the power of benevolence, but they themselves are powerless. They have become agents of a larger social order whose consequences they are unable to recognize. The bonds between man and man can be expressed only through subjection and charity (the act of "love" from the empowered to the powerless).

Believing themselves to be good "fathers," they condemn their "sons" over and over again and console themselves that they have done their best. They are the literary equivalents of the judges who condemn John Brown to hang for his illegal but moral insurrection or who, like Melville's father-in-law, enforce an immoral law such as the Fugitive Slave Act.

Billy Budd: "But for Fate and Ban"

Billy Budd is perhaps Melville's ultimate treatment of the encounter between the Dark Stranger (here metamorphosed into the "light" figure of Billy) and the Captain, whose role has been doubled into those of Claggart and Vere. There is no Hero. The absence of a Hero, of an experiencing self, is part of the reason that *Billy Budd* is in many ways Melville's darkest work (of those I have discussed; it is no darker than *Pierre* or *The Confidence-Man*). The novels we have already looked at end in ways that suggest a lack of ultimate closure: Tom goes back to the ship, but he will jump ship in Tahiti; Redburn goes home, but abandons Harry; White-Jacket and the crew are joined in brotherhood, but the Captain has made them shave their beards; Ahab kills himself and the entire crew, but Queequeg's coffin enables Ishmael to survive. That structural pattern is also true of *Billy Budd*: the Captain executes Billy, but Claggart is dead, Vere himself dies soon after, while Billy lives on in his ballad (a point to which we will return). But the novel gives us no reason to believe that anything will change socially or that any personal change can be effected, since there is no one in the story to respond to the events. It may be that Melville was no longer able to imagine a protagonist as a young sailor; but it also seems likely that he no longer had any illusion that the world might be altered. The Veres will rule, thus allowing the Claggarts their way, and the Billies will die.

Billy Budd is above all a study of repression. All three of the principal characters have transferred energy from one form to another. In Claggart sexual desire for Billy, inexpressible on board ship and on the part of a master-at-arms, is transformed into hatred. For Claggart destruction of Billy is a distorted product of a deep unacknowledgable desire. For Captain Vere an affectionate paternal regard is sacrificed for the sake of a career. A fundamental goodness and desire for order can be expressed only by the suppression of all feeling in the name of authority. Both Claggart and Vere are betrayed by their place in a social order that values control and suppression. The police and the military are devoted to control both internal and external; they require of those under their authority a loss of self and the replacement of personal desire by aggression. They must kill that which threatens their precarious control of self; for that reason murder becomes a kind of suicide. Billy himself also shows the consequences of transferal of energy under repression. His stutter is a physical index of the conflict within himself between speech and silence, the self-enforced suppression of a language of protest. The tongue that should cry out against empressment becomes the arm that strikes the agent of injustice. The sexuality of *Billy Budd* is a sexuality divested of its subversive power: it is the sexual attraction between power and powerlessness, a sado-masochistic drama that contains all its energies and turns them inward. Billy declines to rebel, out of loyalty to a false system, but he dies at the hands of that system in any case. Rebellion is hopeless in this closed world where beauty is simultaneously feared and desired. The destruction of Billy is Claggart's and Vere's attempt to preserve themselves. The intricate pas de trois of these doomed characters serves to remind us of the extent to which military action is a perversion of love. In this homosocial world, charged with sexual potential, only strict control of the homosexual within can prevent a mutiny.

The marriage that stands at the symbolic center of *Moby-Dick*, like the similar relationships that hover, unrealized, around the other novels, is essential to Melville's reconciliation of heart and head, to his achievement of that higher androgynous state described in "After the Pleasure Party." Without the possibility of such a marriage, the innocent Billy is incapable of carrying alone the burden of salvation. He has the self-consciousness, we are told, of a Saint Bernard dog; like that dog he may offer temporary aid but no real means of escape. Billy's beauty makes him a homosexual icon, not a figure in a realized homosexual relationship. His blankness is a kind of slate on which others inscribe their desires. Lacking his own identity, he becomes that which others desire. He is a sexual object, made over by the perceiver. But he is also the figure of the homosexual as victim. His death indicates Melville's failure of belief in the possibility of change.

One should not, however, exaggerate Billy's flaws. He is presented in a number of positive ways that link him to figures from the earlier novels. His mythic associations are with Hercules and Apollo, images of strength and beauty. But he retains few of the attributes of Apollo, except perhaps, by way of Nietzsche, an opposition to a Dionysian element of celebration. He is associated with the archetype of the Handsome Sailor and hence with phallic power—wayfarers render "tribute" to the "black pagod" or idol like the Assyrian priests before the "grand sculptured Bull." But, as Melville suggests, his relationship to the Handsome Sailor is primarily "in aspect" whereas "in nature" there are "important variations" (p. 44). Billy's appearance is of perfect beauty, the union of masculine and feminine, but his acts show little sign that he has achieved that transcendence of sexual difference. The novel's dedication to Jack Chase, the Handsome Sailor of *White-Jacket*, makes Billy's inadequacies clear. Billy is too soft, too weak, and too passive to be considered worthy of the heritage of Jack Chase.

Billy's appeal is pederastic, and he is therefore inadequate as the locus of the erotic energy that Melville felt was necessary to combat tyranny. For pederastic love does nothing to alter the power relationships of heterosexual love; it merely substitutes a powerless boy for a powerless woman. It is not surprising then that both of the authority figures in the novel should be in some sense in love with Billy. He is a tempting figure, but one who does nothing to contradict the order of society. Hence love for him, like the Greek love on which it is modeled, is consistent with a hierarchical society in which slave boys are a perfectly acceptable object of male lust (Billy's link to the African at the beginning of the novella stresses his role as captured slave and renders his love for his master Vere all the more ironic and self-defeating). Melville's task was to make his reader feel the attractiveness of Billy while at the same time recognizing his inadequacies. Melville may himself have felt such an ambivalent response. He seems to have preferred the statue of Antinous in the Villa Albani to all other works of art and even had a cast of Antinous, the beloved of Hadrian, in his room. He clearly fell in love with Hawthorne, although he would later satirize him as a frightened, almost effeminate figure (as Falsgrave in *Pierre*, for instance). But the political context of *Billy Budd* makes it necessary to pass beyond a figure like Billy; and nothing in the story makes that possible. Billy's external beauty is not a sign of spiritual beauty, and so he falsifies both the *Symposium* ideal of ascending love and the Greek aesthetic ideal of a harmony between idea and realization, between content and form. In the archetype of the Handsome Sailor, as established by Melville in the first section, "moral nature" is allied to "physical make" (p. 44). Furthermore, the Handsome Sailor is "intensely black," while Billy has a "rose-tan" complexion (pp. 50, 119). The blue-eyed rosy-cheeked innocent can hardly stand for the values of the Dark Stranger. The introductory passages thus serve to establish an ironic context in which to see Billy, just as the Nelson chapter serves as an ironic context for Vere.

Billy's physical beauty is explicitly linked to that of David, at least in one version of the manuscript: Billy is "goodly to behold"[8] as David is "goodly to look to" (1 Sam. 16:12), just as Claggart's hatred of Billy is a version of Saul's hatred of the David he had once loved ("Saul's visage

perturbedly brooding on the comely young David" [p. 78]), an allusion
introduced to be denied, since "Claggart's was no vulgar form of the
passion." His ability to sing links him to Orpheus—probably as musician
and lyrist a variant of the David figure, whose "harp" is often translated as
"lyre"—but we recall the fate of that earlier Orpheus, Harry. Even as a
figure of Orpheus, Billy seems strangely inadequate. If the quality of his
voice is, as Melville says, "expressive of the harmony within," then his
stutter seems to bespeak some disharmony. Melville in fact calls the stutter
an "organic hesitancy," a deliberately circumlocutory phrase that calls attention to the role of the stutter as an outward sign of an inner failure of
nerve. The degree of innocence that Billy represents simply cannot exist in
the world; indeed it becomes a kind of evil, the inability to ever know or
judge. One is tempted to compare Billy's innocence and its destruction to
James's account of Daisy Miller, but Daisy is willful where Billy is passive.
He does not even recognize, with Bartleby, the power of passivity as a
response to the world. Billy's only song is contained in the four words he
expresses at the moment of his hanging, "God bless Captain Vere!" For
these words there is no stutter, and they are "delivered in the clear melody
of a singing bird on the point of launching from the twig" (p. 123). At
the moment of death, Billy is in total harmony, in total opposition to the
events that have overtaken him. If Billy is to be Orpheus, he must offer us
a greater song than this, a mere "conventional felon's benediction." The
natural imagery of the bird "launching from the twig" is grotesquely at
odds with the actuality of the military execution; it indicates Billy's return
to the nature of which he has always really been a part. Orpheus's power
comes from his ability to cast a spell upon the violence of nature, from the
potential of art to unite nature and a higher intelligence. But Billy's art is
mere birdsong, a conventional phrase that has no power to transform
nature. His metamorphosis is only his return to his proper element. That
Billy represents only nature, a nature without humanity as it were, does
not reduce the condemnation of those who destroy him; Vere and Claggart, like Ahab, must bend nature to their purposes and destroy it in order
to serve themselves. But it does mean that Billy, however appealing, cannot be the "hero," and that the story of which he is "the main figure is no
romance" (p. 53).

Billy is Melville's most reduced version of the Dark Stranger—light
instead of dark, weak instead of strong. The shift in this character, along
with the absence of the Hero, makes the novel one of political despair.
What hope can there be for resistance to unjust authority when there is no
alternative? Billy goes to his death without uttering a single word of
protest, without harboring a single thought of anger against Vere or his

silent shipmates. Can this be the response of White-Jacket who, when facing a flogging, determines whether it is necessary to kill the Captain rather than submit: this final act seems a "privilege, inborn and inalienable" (p. 280)? Or of Steelkilt, the ultimate rebel and true Christ of Melville's vision, who avenges himself without even killing Radney? Unlike his antecedents, Billy goes to his death like a lamb to slaughter. Although the light of the dawn may make the fleecy clouds look like "the fleece of the Lamb of God" (p. 124), the comparison does not ennoble Billy or give his death divine significance. It is one last confirmation of his status as a poor dumb animal, killed for human notions he cannot comprehend. At the same time, it is Melville's final assertion of the complicity of the Church in the ways of the state and its consequent abandonment of any message inherent in the story of Christ's sacrifice. From the missionaries of *Typee* to the chaplain of *Billy Budd* the Church is condemned in terms of the very values it claims to represent: brotherly love and peace. If Billy is Christ, he is nonredemptive. His death leads to no new life and asserts merely the Church's inability to respond to a world in which state power has replaced family order.

Melville's ironic Billy is perhaps one last response to Hawthorne as well. For Billy is clearly modeled on Donatello whose fall into experience Hawthorne seems to have seen as necessary and even beneficial. Innocence destroyed, Melville suggests in return, does not elevate mankind; it only allows those in power to continue to exercise their authority. Melville's Billy shows up the inadequacy of Hawthorne's representation of innocence in a half-animal, half-human creature, with only his androgynous beauty to recommend him. If Hawthorne could use *The Marble Faun* to state his case against Melville and male friendship one last time, Melville in turn could use *Billy Budd* to display the inadequacies of Hawthorne's vision of innocence as well as his failure to understand evil. For if Claggart bears the sign of the serpent that Hawthorne so often employed, he is also the product of repression, a refusal of the sexual that is transformed into a hatred for all that he, by his own refusal, cannot have. That repression too Melville associated with Hawthorne, the nunlike white swan now touched by Amor's fury.

Claggart, "a sort of chief of police" (p. 64), illustrates the transformation of sexual energy when it is placed at the service of authority.[9] Like a chief of police (and we recall that the master-at-arms of *White-Jacket* is compared to Vidocq, the master criminal and child molester become police chief), Claggart exercises authority that is really in the hands of someone else. His physical discipline (represented here by the rattan) enforces laws he does not make, against crimes he himself commits, or would commit. The police authority, as Melville depicts it, is an arm of the state, prepared to lie and distort in order to preserve its power. The rattan that Claggart carries is thus a perfect figure for the repressive authority that relies upon a transformation of the erotic—it is as if Queequeg's pipe became a tomahawk again. The sexual potential of the rattan is clear in the episode of the spilled soup: Claggart was about to "ejaculate something hasty," but instead "playfully tapped him from behind with his rattan" (p. 72). The playful tap of an instrument of punishment calls attention to this bivalent figure: ejaculate or strike, play or punish, cock or rattan.

Claggart's desire for Billy thus becomes the desire to sodomize Billy (and, in the social context, to sodomize means to exert power). Claggart reconverts dispersed sexual energy (Billy's spilled soup) into directed phallic aggression. As in *White-Jacket*, punishment in *Billy Budd* is the equivalent of physical aggression: whipping is a kind of male rape (including ceremonial undressing) that aims at humiliation as a means to the assertion or maintenance of power. Yet the desires in *Billy Budd* are inverted, so that Claggart's desire for Billy is not only a desire to hurt Billy, but also a desire to *provoke* Billy, so that *he* (Claggart) can be raped by Billy. His false accusation achieves this purpose by finally provoking Billy to raise his arm. At last erect, Billy lacks the means of ejaculation, so verbal force must be replaced by physical, as sexual energy by aggressive. When Billy strikes Claggart, he in some strange way fulfills Claggart's desire: Claggart dies instantly, at last possessed by that which he has sought to possess. He leaves behind, of course, his tongue, the agent of his posthumous victory over Billy. Throughout the novella, speech is the means of power, whether in the insinuating, snake-like hisses of Claggart or the oily subtleties of Vere: Billy of course lacks speech. His stutter is a sign of his powerlessness, an inability at once sexual and verbal. It sprays words without direction, like the soup that Billy spills. Such a generalized *ejaculatio praecox* prevents him from ever employing the power inherent in his beauty, and of course is given form again in the too-quick arm. Billy's sexuality suffuses everything but is too diffuse to make a difference. It is the sexuality that can be employed to divert political energies. Billy has been removed from the *Rights-of-Man*; his fate demonstrates the hopelessness, indeed the destructiveness, of a sexuality removed from politics.

Envy of Billy's physical beauty, desire for that which he cannot have but by his own gestures acknowledges he wants—these forces cumulate in Claggart and are transformed into the hatred that is the opposite side of the coin of love. "But for fate and ban" (p. 88) Claggart "could even have loved Billy." But the moments in which Claggart seems to realize this, in which his expression is one of "soft yearning," are "evanescent," and he quickly returns to his "immitigable look," like a "wrinkled walnut." By his refusal of that yearning, Claggart loses all his own spirit, and what might have been his natural expression of affection becomes instead the venomous kiss of the serpent. Only a few years later Oscar Wilde would write, "Each man kills the thing he loves." So in Melville's darkest mood he recognized the intricate relationship between love and hatred and what seemed like the inevitable destruction of love by a system that needed to make chiefs of police out of its greatest villains. The Claggart/Billy relationship is the only thing that could have altered the bleak outcome of the story or have provided some possibility for the reconciliation of cultural oppositions (Melville located the prototypes of Claggart and Billy near each other in the Capitoline Museum, in the figures of Tiberius and Antinous)[10]. Claggart's refusal is not only the rejection of a "banned" love, although it is that, but it is also the larger social process by which all instincts of love are transformed into those of hatred in the name of service to the state and the engines of war. Vere, too, seems a potential lover whose love is repressed. Humorless, undemonstrative, he has made war into a "science" (p. 60) and law into a series of regulations. Although apparently fond of Billy who, he thinks, "in the nude might have posed for a statue of young Adam before the Fall" (p. 94), and even considering him "for promotion to a place that would more frequently bring him under his own observation" (p. 95), he does not allow personal affection (or lust) to overcome a strict adherence to what he claims to be the "forms." Much has been made of Vere's love for Billy as expressed in his stateroom at the time of Billy's sentence, but every action alluded to there is preceded by "may have." Melville is already shifting his tale toward its concern with the means by which history operates to sentimentalize and assimilate by a process of rewriting that becomes explicit at the end of *Billy Budd*. If Vere loves Billy, it is a love that kills in the name of discipline.

If the sexual and psychological drama of the novel is located in the conflict between Billy and Claggart, the political drama is located in the conflict between Billy and Vere. That drama is also partly psychological, since Vere is no mere villain but a portrait of a reasonable man in the service of an unreasoning office. And his service of what he perceives to be his duty in fact exceeds any actual obligations. If Vere were evil in the way Claggart is, we would be faced with a story of primarily psychological import; because Vere is "normal" and yet very much like Claggart, we are faced with a story that deals with a permanent political dilemma: Can the good person serve the state? It is on the issue of Vere that Melville criticism has split most remarkably. The critics who see Ahab as the hero of *Moby-Dick*, in more than a technical sense, are still a small minority. But it appears that a majority of readers have found Vere to be the hero and locus of value in *Billy Budd*. Such a misunderstanding is frightening, not so much for what it says about the ability to deal with the text (and Melville did create problems by writing a text without a hero)[11] as for what it says about the society of which Melville had already so despaired. *Billy Budd* is the first Melville text in which the Captain is given real psychological depth, but his place in a hierarchical structure of power in which mutiny—the revolt of the children against the father—is the greatest danger renders him incapable of realizing whatever potential for love or wisdom he may possess.

Nothing that we know about the role of the Captain from the earlier works would lead us to believe that Melville would create a captain who represents the moral perspective of the author: every Captain in Melville is corrupt, a tyrant, or a madman. But it is of course possible that Melville came to reject everything he had once believed. Let us look then more carefully at Melville's characterization of Vere. He is a snob. With a "leaning" toward "everything intellectual," he always takes to sea a "newly replenished library, compact but of the best." What texts? Those books that "every *serious* mind of *superior* order occupying any *active* post of authority in the world *naturally* inclines" toward [my emphasis]. His conservatism is not the product of careful reflection on new ideas, but instead "a dike against those invading waters of novel opinion social, political and otherwise" (p. 62). The pomposity of his character is accurately embodied in the language of these passages, language that is employed as a kind of *style indirect libre*, echoing Vere's conceptions of himself and his stilted, self-satisfied phraseology. He is also a tyrant, exercising total political authority, compared by Melville to Peter the Great (p. 103) and his palace intrigues. His speeches to the court are masterpieces of portrayal, illustrating the false protestations and self-proclaimed honor of the prosecuting attorney. His rhetoric here shifts tone and subject with the ease of *Hamlet*'s Claudius. But at its heart it is the rhetoric of Ahab: "You see then, whither, prompted by duty and the law, I steadfastly drive" (p. 113). The participial clause is enough to assert his honor but hardly enough to disguise the aggressive energy that it seeks to clothe in virtue.

Vere's behavior in the court is crucial to an evaluation of him, for if he is to be valued, it must be as the man of law, through what Milton Stern has called "his sacrifice of self to the necessities of moral responsibility historically defined."[12] What is important to note about Melville's portrayal of Vere is that he betrays the very code he claims to believe in. It is not even necessary to accept the idea of a moral code higher than military justice (although I am certain that Melville did so) in order to condemn Vere.

Revolution may be a legitimate fear, but does it justify the suspension of legal procedure? And if Vere acts only out of a justified fear of mutiny, why not act on that basis instead of cloaking his behavior in legal self-righteousness? Surely the first obligation of a court is to determine evidence; that this court never does. Vere is the accuser, the witness, and the judge; he is even the defense counsel at moments. No witnesses are heard; no attempt is ever made to determine the truth of Claggart's accusation. Of course the fact that the accusation is false does not alter the fact that Billy killed Claggart, but it does determine a great deal about motive and justification. Indeed, it is ironic, as C. N. Manlove has pointed out, that Vere's refusal to consider Billy's intentions argues against any consideration of Vere's intentions when he violates legal procedure.[13] It is hardly the function of courts to make mere determination of facts; as Leonard Casper has pointed out, Vere's rulings make the court function as a coroner's jury, which has no power to sentence anyone.[14] And some investigation might determine whether or not mutiny is really likely on board the *Bellipotent*; the issue is important, since it is Vere's assumption of the danger of mutiny that justifies his suspension of proper procedure, although no effort whatever is made to examine that assumption. Vere has decided Billy's fate before the court meets, and he uses his power to manipulate the court's decision. The trial is a sham, the pretense of justice and not justice itself.

Melville's language makes the situation clear. By what amounts to "jugglery of circumstances," the guilty and the innocent have been reversed. Claggart is only the "apparent victim," while Billy is in fact "victimize[d]." But this is not the appearance of things "in the light of that martial code," or "navally regarded." The question of "essential right and wrong" is too "primitive" (p. 103) to be used as a basis for decision. Melville is not suggesting that essential decisions must await divine justice; he is sardonically portraying what passes for justice under a system of military law. After all, all but the most fundamentalist of Christians accept the necessity of striving for justice, even if they believe that final justice must await eternity; and the word "primitive" can only be applied to the question of right or wrong in an ironic sense.

Vere's own language is a parody of judicial argument, marked by the substitution of the abstraction for the concrete. We know that Vere is capable of adopting other rhetorics, but his use of this discourse of law is Melville's depiction of the corruption of the office: in the courtroom one is faced with the temptation to speak, and hence to think, legally and so betray one's humanity: "Quite apart from any conceivable motive *actuating* the master-at-arms, and *irrespective* of the *provocation* to the blow, a martial court must needs *in the present case* confine its attention to *the blow's consequence, which consequence* justly is *to be deemed* not otherwise than as the striker's deed" (p. 107; I have italicized the most striking examples of legalese). All of these words amount to saying nothing more than that Billy struck Claggart. It is not possible to imagine that Melville would cast as a hero a man who could so abuse the language. But he could imagine that a man of ambition would use such language to assist himself on his way to a glorious career and that such language would be an effective means of concealing, perhaps even from himself, the immorality of what he does.

At other places Vere argues in terms of "paramount obligations," the very phrase ironic in that it means for him professional responsibility and not moral responsibility. Here he weighs his duties in a series of on-the-one-hand, on-the-other-hand contrasts that again echo Claudius: "though . . . as sailors, yet as the King's officers," "warm hearts" and "heads that should be cool," "private conscience" and "imperial" conscience, "though as their fellow creatures . . . , yet as navy officers" (pp. 110–12). The final contrast can leave no doubt of Vere's abdication of moral responsibility. No one can ever maintain an obligation higher than that to "their fellow creatures," since to do so means to deny one's place as a human being, to make one's political position more important than one's humanity. Vere's justifications for himself echo the reasoning of Melville's father-in-law, Lemuel Shaw, whose decision in the Sims case required the enforcement of the Fugitive Slave Act. Shaw thereby rejected his own prior adherence to natural rights in favor of codified law. A major defense of Vere argues that he represents a "higher ethic" than "justice to the individual," namely "the claims of civilized society."[15] This argument, of course, begs the question of determining who speaks for "civilized society." But it also misrepresents the novel, because Vere cannot be said to speak for society, except insofar as he dictates the microcosmic society of the *Bellipotent*. Vere's decision to hold the court is contrary to law and to the opinion of his officers. It corresponds only to his own desires. Far from establishing a higher social order, Vere imposes the rule of the individual (himself) over social justice. His actions have been compared to the ethical code of Plotinus Plinlimmon in *Pierre*[16]. The analogy is astonishing as an attempt to persuade us of Melville's agreement with Vere. Plinlimmon is one of the many characters in *Pierre* who satirize some element of Hawthorne; he represents the false absolutist, the man who preaches a high truth while secretly accepting the corruption of the world and indulging himself. If Vere is in any way like Plinlimmon, then he is surely one of Melville's nastiest characters. Both of them claim allegiance to a noble code of behavior as a front to deceive others; as Plinlimmon is a false prophet, Vere is a false judge.

The society of *Billy Budd* is corrupt, since power creates greed. The weak serve the strong so that they may profit from them. The Church has been turned into an arm of the state and hence becomes a collaborator in murder (the execution of prisoners) and war. Over and over again Melville has called attention to the role of the military chaplain, who by accepting that post betrays the Church to which he claims allegiance. One cannot serve both God and Mammon. The chaplain on the *Bellipotent* is "the minister of Christ though receiving his stipend from Mars"; by accepting such service he "lends the sanction of the religion of the meek to that which practically is the abrogation of everything but brute Force" (pp. 120, 122). The Church, which ought to oppose power, abandons its faith so that it can share in power. The "war contractors" have an interest in war, since they have "an anticipated portion of the harvest of death" (p. 119). Having invested their money in preparation for war, and in the production of the instruments of war, their financial motive leads them to encourage war. Peace might bring financial ruin. As the Church collaborates and the capitalists invest, those involved in the hierarchy of the state seek their own advancement. Vere, that double of Claggart, is driven by "the most secret of all passions, ambition" (p. 129). But, as Claggart is never able to profit from his currying of favor with higher authority by denouncing Billy, since he is killed by Billy, so Vere does not live long enough to attain to "the fulness of fame," since he is killed in battle by the French shortly after Billy's execution. The deaths of the two men who might have gained by the death of Billy add a final turn of the ironic screw: all that killing, and not even ambition is served.

Both Vere's defenders and his attackers have pointed to the chapter on Lord Nelson as a model by which to judge Vere. One school argues that Nelson is an example of "supreme heroism"; another claims that although Nelson represents "the ideal version of the governing principle," Vere is "unable to emulate this ideal."[17] But the issue is not whether or not Vere measures up to Nelson: Nelson is a false standard from the beginning. One would be surprised if it were otherwise: a loss of faith in Nelson is one of the most important of Redburn's deceptions in Liverpool. At the base of the statue of Nelson he sees "four naked figures in chains" which he could never look at "without being involuntarily reminded of four African slaves in the market-place" (p. 155). Nelson is thus identified as a hero of the imperial venture, and that venture is one of the enslavement of the nonwhite world. Slavery is at the heart of *Billy Budd*. Billy himself is linked to the "black pagod," and his removal from the *Rights-of-Man* is a synecdochic re-creation of the enslavement of the blacks and their loss of rights. They too live under a martial system, virtually deprived of all legal rights, in the name of law (i.e., the protection of property and authority). In his account of Nelson in *Billy Budd*, Melville addresses the issue of Nelson's alleged heroism and sees it as the expression of a desire for glory. Melville pretends to answer the "utilitarians" who claim that Nelson was imprudent in appearing on deck in an "ornate publication of his person." Not so, says Melville, tongue in cheek, "an excessive love of glory" is the first virtue of a military man. It is a defense that condemns by its own absurd terms. Melville concludes the digression on Nelson by an interesting comment that develops the metaphor of "publication" and links Nelson's actions to aesthetic practice: ". . . if thus to have adorned himself for the altar and the sacrifice were indeed vainglory, then affectation and fustian is each more heroic line in the great epics and dramas, since in such lines the poet but embodies in verse those exaltations of sentiment that a nature like Nelson, the opportunity being given, vitalizes into acts" (p. 58). Nelson's is the heroism of epic posturing and dramatic self-aggrandizement; it is the historic analogue to the rhetoric of Ahab. *Billy Budd* is antiheroic in theme and language. In it Melville abandons the language of excess for a plain style appropriate to a heroless world. Society has created the model of Nelson as hero at the price of human liberty; Vere's desire to emulate it can only bring disaster to himself and to others.

    Following the execution of Billy, Vere attempts to restore order on the ship and justifies himself with the words, "with mankind forms, measured forms, are everything; and that is the import couched in the story of Orpheus with his lyre spellbinding the wild denizens of the wood" (p. 128). The thought of Vere as Orpheus—when in fact if there is an Orpheus on this ship it must be Billy—should be ludicrous enough. In any case, the lyre has lost its efficacy: neither Billy nor Vere can transform nature by the power of art. But several other elements of irony are also present. Vere is maintaining not the "forms" but a mere appearance of form. As Mary Foley has pointed out, Vere is in constant conflict with time: he judges the case sooner than it should be (it should be held for the admiral), and the execution means the events of the next day are an hour ahead of schedule.[18] The court meets in his stateroom, hardly a neutral place, and he himself testifies from the weather side (that is, as the Captain and not as a witness), an action that may be "apparently trivial" (p. 105) but that is nonetheless a deliberate violation of the "forms." As Richard Stavig describes his actions, Vere's "stipulated conditions thus make the 'decision' of the court the merest formality. Vere's choice had been made earlier; his problem now is merely to select four members of the court who can comprehend the significance of his conditions, and then to present them in such a way that they are perfectly clear."[19] Vere uses the appearance of the "forms" to conceal his own violations of both their letter and their spirit. His motive for doing so may be partially valid (that is, he may actually believe in the possibility of mutiny), but he appeals to the "forms" only as a cover.

Many readers make a direct connection between Vere's reference to the "forms" and Melville's allusion in the following chapter to "the symmetry of form in pure fiction," and Hayford and Sealts in their definitive edition even point to Melville's poem "Greek Architecture," with its reference to a respect for inherent "Form" (note to leaf 333). However, the difference between Vere's plural and Melville's singulars must be considered. It is totally misguided to connect Vere's appeal to "measured forms" to a classical concept of "Form." As Melville presents the latter idea in "Greek Architecture," he describes an art that is in harmony with nature, rejecting the "wilfulness" of the individual Romantic artist who imposes his ideas on nature for a response in "reverence for the Archetype." This classical view is consistent with a nineteenth-century concept of organic form, since organic form is derived from nature, the archetype, and not from the human will. Words connected with "form" are never used in this sense in *Billy Budd*: Billy is to be judged "formally" and not by nature (p. 103); our world is one of "formalized humanity," from which affection is banished (p. 115). The word "measured" is also used in a negative context: when Claggart accuses Billy he approaches with "measured step" (p. 98). In *Billy Budd*, then, "measured" means calculated, and "forms" are human impositions on nature. This is not the "measure" or the "form" of Greek aesthetics.[20] Nor is Melville's acknowledgment that *Billy Budd* may not achieve "the symmetry of form attainable in pure fiction" (p. 128) a criticism of the work; Melville's aim is the "truth uncompromisingly told" which "will always have its ragged edges." The contrast between "symmetry" and "truth" is one that is important for *Billy Budd*, of course, since it is an aesthetic equivalent of the contrast between the "forms" and justice. Can any reader of *Moby-Dick* really believe that Melville valued symmetry above all else? above truth? Melville's art is always "ragged" because he will not accept the falsification necessary to achieve the illusion of symmetry. Because life is manifold, its representation in art must be flexible enough to capture that diversity.

As we have seen in all of Melville's works, his characteristic technique for achieving that representation of diversity is the mixing of genres. That formal solution is employed in *Billy Budd* as well. We have already looked at the chapter on Nelson and seen how this historical interlude functions as a doubly ironic foil for Vere (Vere can never be Nelson, but then Nelson is not worth being anyway) and as a commentary on the Melvillean aesthetics of dissemination. The death of Billy is followed by five such digressions, or five alternate endings. All of them are attempts, as Mary Foley has said, "to apply some law or pattern to the novel's events" in contrast to the "organic form" the novel already possesses.[21] All are as false aesthetically as they are false in content. Like the classifications of "cetology," they cannot represent the truth. The first of them is a conversation of the Purser and the Surgeon that echoes the gravediggers' scene in *Hamlet*. Like that scene it shocks by its sharp contrast of vulgarity and beauty, of scientific knowledge and the fact of death. The bawdy humor about the absence of a final ejaculation as Billy was hanged calls attention to the sexual theme and confirms Billy's lack of the seminal power that could at once resist authority and create a new erotic order while at the same time demonstrating the inability of a sexual metaphor to say all there is about Billy: surely he is more than an orgasm, which is in turn more than the discourse of science will allow in its attempt to use language to mystify and to transform the multiple human experience into an analogy that links the body to a malfunctioning engine—in the Surgeon's words it is "a mechanical spasm in the muscular system" (p. 124). Like the discussion of *Hamlet*'s gravediggers, their mordant humor reflects on the world around them and on the pretentiousness of science and its inability to deal with human experience. They even deal in a little Greek, discussing "*euthanasia*," which they apparently take to mean suicide. Just as the gravedigger's false Latin, *se offendendo* for self-defense, turns out to be meaningful (suicide, presumably, is an offense, not a defense), the false Greek is not only a joke at the expense of the pseudo-learned but a hint at Melville's meanings. *Euthanasia* was just acquiring its new sense (as a death inflicted as an act of kindness), and Melville was able to play on the ambiguity inherent in the term.[22]

The second digression is devoted to the response of the men on the *Bellipotent*. Despite their love for Billy, they can offer only a "muffled murmur" for they, like him, are "inarticulate"; their murmur is indeed echoed by that of the birds who fly to the site where Billy's body has fallen into the sea, looking for food. It is one of the book's darkest moments, for the men are nothing more than animals, their highest goal food, whatever impulse they might once have had to resistance having been eroded by years of "martial discipline." They save their own necks, and procure their own meals, by following orders. In that they do no more than Billy had tried to do, and his failure to achieve immunity through following orders is a lesson that never touches them. When he first sees the novice flogged,

Billy's response is not anger or revenge but only the resolve never to "make himself liable" to such punishment (p. 68). Billy is incapable of recognizing that injustice committed against one person is injustice committed against everyone. There is thus a small amount of poetic justice that the crew like him chooses to follow orders rather than rebel. Sauve qui peut.

A similar justice of sorts is achieved by Vere in the third digression, in which his death at sea is recounted. One suspects that there is more symmetry in these digressions than Melville had allowed; seeming formlessness turns out to be true form. Claggart, the villain, is given a hero's death in the newspaper account that forms the fourth digression. Almost every fact in the account is wrong—Billy is said to have stabbed Claggart, who is termed "respectable and discreet," and Billy is thought to be an alien and Claggart a patriot (p. 130). The account of Claggart's death is a wonderful depiction of the ways in which heroes are manufactured. Perhaps one day there will be a statue to Claggart to match that to Nelson. The final digression, and the final falsehood, is the ballad, "Billy in the Darbies." Several critics have seen the ballad as the novel's most affirmative statement. Ray B. West argues that the ballad "represents Melville's final expression of faith in mankind—faith in the ability of the common man to see beyond the misrepresentations of evil, however disguised,"[23] and Ray B. Browne sees Billy triumphing through the ballad, in a "resounding affirmation of belief in the ultimate triumph of the Rights of Man and of democracy."[24] Despite their Fourth of July rhetoric Melville does nothing of the kind. He concludes with a final poem that is a vivid demonstration of the common man's inability to understand. Melville concludes *Billy Budd* in the belief that tyranny will continue to triumph because no one will ever have the courage to fight back.

Many critics, I believe, simply want Melville to come round to a happier end to his life—they want the "symmetry" of "pure fiction" in which everything is reconciled. They want a Melville who was unhappy and often bitter but who really believed in America and its future. The truth is that Melville grew increasingly more pessimistic about the future of America and indeed of all society, and he gave expression in *Billy Budd* to his gravest doubts about man's ability to survive in more than a state of animal-like acceptance. As Karl Zink has put it, the distortion of the ballad "betrays subtly the undiscriminating docility of the pliant crew."[25] They have found in Billy another hero, not the political hero for whom one makes statues but the popular hero for whom one sings ballads. But popular mythmaking is as false as political hero-making. The iconoclast of *Pierre* still believes that people must live by truth, not by the false portraits set up to honor the past. Nothing in the ballad conveys anything about Billy's life or makes anything significant of his death. The process of ballad-making is one that acts to defuse the social energy of rebellion; it is always permissible to eulogize a dead hero and preferable from the point of view of power to finding a live leader. The ballad-makers serve the state as much as the war contractors or the chaplains: as Melville wrote of Charles Dibdin in *White-Jacket*, "these songs are pervaded by a true Mohammedan sensualism; a reckless acquiescence in fate, and an implicit, unquestioning, dog-like devotion to whoever may be lord and master. Dibdin was a man of genius; but no wonder Dibdin was a government pensioner at £200 per annum" (p. 383). It is the values inculcated by songs like Dibdin's that create a man like Billy, an innocent prepared to die for the king and bless his executioner. His song, "As for my life, 'tis the King's," cited by Melville in *Billy Budd* (p. 55), is a perfect motto for the wasted self-sacrifice of Billy. The ballad is the last element (or the first, considering its composition) in the construction of a society ruled by the ambitious, policed by the vicious, and peopled by the mindless. Melville's testament is neither one of acceptance nor one of resistance; it is the testament of despair.[26]

Without a viable model of male friendship, Melville could not envision an alternative to his grim picture of society. Without love could there be change? Melville wanted Billy to prevail.[27] At moments, I believe, he wanted that desperately. He did not want to believe in his own dark vision. Surely a beautiful young man might come along and change everything. But however much Melville's heart yearned for that beautiful young man, he knew he would have no mind to share with Melville, no heart to be a companion to Melville's most intimate self. And he did not really believe that he could ever come again. And so Melville had only memory—and death. The last words of the ballad, with which *Billy Budd* began, represent Eros and Thanatos finally reconciled in the embrace of Death. The Golden Isles had become what in a sense they had always been—the islands of the dead. There the "shades" of John Marr and his friends might "twine" and "entwine" once more.

Almost fifty years earlier Melville had written his first novels in a form that led many of their readers to take them for accurate scientific accounts of reality; in their critique of the expansionist society of the time they express Melville's anger at America and his search for a simultaneous political and literary alternative. The search for that alternative would occupy his attention during the following years, through the creation of *Moby-Dick*. The failure of that novel, and the failure of American idealism, as evidenced by the Civil War, made it impossible for Melville to sustain his hopeful vision, even as an alternative. *Billy Budd* makes it clear that in a world at war there can be no place for love. It also makes it clear that beauty alone is not redemptive; indeed because it lacks speech it must always be condemned to misunderstanding and failure.

Billy Budd concludes with simultaneous absolute closure, in that all three major actors are dead, and literary anticlosure, in that the tale ends with multiple versions of telling, none of them adequate to comprehend the experience itself. In Barbara Johnson's words, the ending of *Billy Budd* "empt[ies] the ending of any privileged control over sense."[28] As in *Moby-Dick*, Melville is concerned by the inability of art to depict accurately, since it must run the danger of imposing a falsifying order on experience. However, Melville's position, unlike that of some modern deconstructionists, is that there is indeed an experience, no matter how hard it may be to capture. It is for this reason that he places his emphasis not on the futility of art but on the need for a "ragged" art of truth over a "symmetrical" art of falsification. *Billy Budd* enacts the way in which love is repeatedly transformed into death, a process parallel to the transformation of natural right into state order. Slavery, injustice, and repression remained facts of life for Melville, facts that he no longer found the means to combat.

Reading Schopenhauer in his last years, Melville apparently came to believe in the necessity of transfiguring the self.[29] Only in the annihilation of the personal self could human beings find rest. His view thus turned toward death, but a death that was now fully eroticized. There, among the shades, malice might truly be reconciled. Without the elimination of the will, the world was condemned to eternal repetition. The violence of Billy's gesture is a sign of his inability to transcend himself and thus of the dangers inherent in any attempt to confront will with will. Billy dies not as a triumphant Christ, but rather as a self disintegrating into the primal waters of the nonself. Melville still loved Billy, the direct descendant of all his heroes, but his view of society had so altered that Billy was divested of all capacity for change. Queequeg also undergoes a sacrificial death, of course, but his is directly linked to personal affection and to the survival of Ishmael. Billy dies because he is an infant (that is, literally speechless) and because he is the object of unacknowledgable desire. His death offers life to no one. As Irving Howe has put it, *Billy Budd* was "written from Melville's weary disenchantment with the radical utopianism, the gay anarchism of his youthful years, and [is] thereby a work in which the vision of youth is embodied in a figure at once pure and helpless, angelic and speechless, loved and doomed."[30] The transformation of Marnoo and Queequeg into Billy amounts to a radical defusing of political and erotic energy, and the shift of attention from the Hero to the Captain makes the dilemma one of the employment of power rather than of the resistance to power. Captain Vere indeed engages our sympathy, but only because we know so clearly that he can only save himself by embracing Billy; and that his position as well as his character will never permit him to do. Body and mind thus remain permanently severed, and Billy's effeminacy becomes weakness rather than the triumphant androgyny it once betokened.

The power of the false narratives at the end of *Billy Budd* is the power of assimilation, the ability of a society to make history over again in its own image. Erotic energy, Melville knew, would be co-opted for public consumption and transformed into defused legends of heroic action. Nonetheless, he left behind a final work that tried once more to tell the truth, to leave behind, if only in the form of defeat, a tale that could bear witness to the power of eros and its conflict with authority. *Billy Budd* confirms Melville's final view that the state, in its benign form of justice (Vere) or its malign form of police power (Claggart), could only perceive love as a threatening force that would ultimately lead to mutiny. Power depends, in *Billy Budd*, on the suppression of eros. Male friendship, once a potent force to counteract the arbitrary authority of the Captain, has now gone underground. Sexuality now exists in the sly innuendo rather than in the bold affirmation of *Moby-Dick*. Feared even as it becomes harmless, sexuality persists only in its inverted form of hatred or its sublimated form of regret. The tale that expresses this vision can only be one that trails off into silence.

Billy Budd appears to be less centrally concerned with sexuality than the other, earlier novels that we have examined. But in fact it sees sexuality in the broadest possible terms. The novel is filled with an awareness of the ways in which patriarchal structures must control sexuality. The exertion of authority requires the suppression of the erotic. *Billy Budd*, although lacking female characters, is deeply aware of the need of male authority to suppress the female, just as masculine authority suppresses the feminine. Vere's execution of Billy is his final attempt to rid himself of anything that might be soft, gentle, and feminine; like Ahab's refusal of Starbuck's love, it is a final act that leads directly to his destruction, while at the same time creating for the reader a poignant awareness of the degree to which these men have come close to acknowledging a fundamental androgyny by daring to embrace another man. Refusing this gesture of reconciliation, they affirm the perpetual tyranny of man over woman, white over black, society over nature. Billy's homosexual figure of integration is lost, even as the final ballad betrays its memory by transforming him into the heterosexual admirer of "Bristol Molly." So too Melville may have known what history would make of him.

Coda

The outline of Melville's career suggests a curve remarkably similar to that of his contemporary Richard Wagner. These two giants of nineteenth-century thought have much in common, of course, including the magnitude of their conceptions and the overwhelming effort to find forms adequate to those conceptions. Both *Moby-Dick* and *Der Ring des Nibelungen* are remarkable creations that mirror grandiose dreams of power and envision their apocalyptic resolution. Melville and Wagner begin their careers in the analysis of society and the search for another, almost utopian world. These early stages are infused with the spirit of 1848, with a search for a political change equivalent to the search for a social renewal of a Hellenistic spirit. Then, in a second stage for both Melville and Wagner, the emphasis is placed on the role of personal love, in which eros takes on the role of the major force running counter to the dominant ethos of force and violence. Finally, both artists, alike under the influence of Schopenhauer, see love only as a means to the ultimate renunciation of the world. Love contains the seeds of that change, of course, but love itself must be transcended. The great lovers of these two men's works point the way: Queequeg gives his coffin over to Ishmael, in a perfect act of self-overcoming, as Brünnhilde walks into the flames, enabling the gold to be purified and restored to the Rhine from which it was first stolen. Only by the self-elected death, Wagner and Melville seem to say, can humanity's continual striving be ended and the curse of greed be undone. The Rhine flows over the fire, like the sea over the *Pequod*, or over the body of Billy, and nature has finally regained dominion.

Melville's final stage brought him to the end of a lifelong search for a way to repudiate the power-lust of Western man. The places that once seemed to offer an alternative, like Typee, turn out to be themselves spoilt. Place then gives way to the mind, site of human love and affection, in the search for a restored spirit of fraternity that can combat the aggressive energies of repression and so free the body to the celebration of its own sensuality. But the love in which Melville invested so much hope was tied to the body and hence mortal; and physical love could offer no resistance to spiritual evil, which could trap it every time in the clever language of seduction and judgment. Melville's hope in the end turned to another world, in which purified bodies might at last be reunited, purged of their dross, and twined in the ecstasy of the restoration of wholeness. Faced with the inability to change the world, Melville turned his face away. His legacy remains a remarkable imaginative vision—breathtaking in its scope and in its audacity—that dared to question most of the assumptions of the society he inhabited and to offer love as the only response to the power of evil.

The male couple was the preferred form in which Melville invested his hope for the creation of a subversive form of love that could counteract power. But his lovers are part of the same world as Tristan and Isolde or Siegfried and Brünnhilde; like them, they embrace in a love that ultimately annihilates power and sends Valhalla or the *Pequod* toppling. Their apocalypses are visions of an end that is simultaneously a beginning; but their central spirits have passed out of the world of generation. Dying, they now enter into a greater life, leaving behind them the hope that, for those few who survive the annihilation of the world, recognition of human sympathy may yet offer a means of redemption. Suffering of one must become the suffering of all if the cycle of pain is ever to be broken; this was part of Melville's work as early as *Redburn*, but only in *Moby-Dick* did he contemplate the eternal battle of love and death, sympathy and power. In *Billy Budd* he concluded that the world could not be changed, would not even know the horrors committed in the name of order and authority, and so he ended his search by embracing the death of the self.

Notes

Preface

1. Unpublished letter, June 15, [1922], Hart Crane to Wilbur Underwood, Beinecke Library, Yale University, New Haven, Conn.
2. Hart Crane to Yvor Winters, October 5, 1926, in Thomas Parkinson, ed., *Hart Crane and Yvor Winters: Their Literary Correspondence* (Berkeley: University of California Press, 1978), p. 11.
3. Susan Sontag, "What's Happening in America," in *Styles of Radical Will* (New York: Farrar, Straus & Giroux, 1969), p. 195.

Introduction

1. Leslie Fiedler, *Love and Death in the American Novel*, rev. ed. (New York: Stein and Day, 1966), p. 12.
2. Erik Erikson, *Childhood and Society* (New York: Norton, 1950).
3. Fiedler, *Love and Death*, p. 366.
4. Exceptions include Loren Baritz's chapter on Melville in *City on a Hill* (New York: Wiley, 1964), pp. 271–331, and Michael Rogin's article, "Herman Melville: State, Civil Society, and the American 1848," *Yale Review* 69 (Autumn 1979): 72–88, followed by his book, *Subversive Genealogy: The Politics and Art of Herman Melville* (New York: Knopf, 1983).
5. This point is made very effectively by Ann Douglas, in her *The Feminization of American Culture* (New York: Knopf, 1977), pp. 290–94.
6. F. O. Matthiessen, *American Renaissance: Art and Experience in the Age of Emerson and Whitman* (New York: Oxford University Press, 1941), p. 455.
7. David H. Hirsch, "The Dilemma of the Liberal Intellectual: Melville's Ishmael," *Texas Studies in Language and Literature* 5 (Summer 1963): 169.
8. Roland Barthes, *Le Plaisir du Texte* (Paris: Le Seuil, 1973), pp. 17, 105.
9. Carroll Smith-Rosenberg, "The Female World of Love and Ritual: Relations between Women in Nineteenth-Century America," *Signs: Journal of Women in Culture and Society* 1 (Autumn 1975): 27–28. See also Lillian Faderman on the

"romantic friendship," *Surpassing the Love of Men: Romantic Friendship and Love between Women from the Renaissance to the Present* (New York: Morrow, 1981), and George Chauncey, Jr., "From Sexual Inversion to Homosexuality: Medicine and the Changing Conceptualization of Female Deviance," *Salmagundi* 58–59 (Fall 1982–Winter 1983): 114–46.

10. Janet Todd, *Women's Friendship in Literature* (New York: Columbia University Press, 1980), p. 2.

11. Edwin Haviland Miller, *Melville* (New York: George Braziller, 1975). I address some of its flaws in my review, "Billy Budd's Stutter," *The Nation*, February 14, 1976, pp. 184–86. For the larger issues raised by this kind of criticism, see also my essay, "Criticizing the Critics: A Gay Perspective," *Gay Sunshine*, no. 35 (Winter 1978): 24–25.

12. In Douglas's words, Melville "conceived masculinity, as Fuller understood feminism, essentially as resistance to sentimentalism, as an effort at a genuinely political and philosophical life" (p. 294).

13. G. J. Barker-Benfield, *The Horrors of the Half-Known Life: Male Attitudes toward Women and Sexuality in Nineteenth-Century America* (New York: Harper & Row, 1976), p. 12. Barker-Benfield is commenting on Ik Marvel's *Reveries of a Bachelor*, a very popular nineteenth-century text.

14. Newton Arvin, *Herman Melville* (New York: William Sloane, 1950), p. 180.

Chapter 1

1. Sir James G. Frazer, "The Belief in Immortality among the Marquesans," in *The Belief in Immortality and the Worship of the Dead*, 2 vols. (London: Macmillan, 1913), 2:328–74. J. J. Bachofen, *Antiquarische Briefen*, Nachlass [1880], in *Gesammelte Werke*, 8: 493ff., cited by Hermann Augustin, "J. J. Bachofen und Herman Melville: Ein Hinweis," *Schweizer Monatshefte* 46 (1967): 1128–31.

2. Charles R. Anderson, *Melville in the South Seas* (1939; rpt. New York: Dover, 1966).

3. This point was first made by James E. Miller, Jr., in "Melville's Search for Form," *Bucknell Review* 8 (December 1959): 266. It has been made more recently by Janet Giltrow, "Speaking Out: Travel and Structure in Herman Melville's Early Narratives," *American Literature* 52 (March 1980): 18–32, but she gives too little sense of Melville's use of the travel narrative in the construction of a fictional form.

4. Newton Arvin, *Herman Melville* (New York: William Sloane, 1950), pp. 56–57. Jacob Stockinger's essay, "Homotextuality: A Proposal," suggests the significance of travel literature as a form of gay self-discovery (in Louie Crew, ed., *The Gay Academic* [Palm Springs, Calif.: ETC, 1978], pp. 135–51; see section iv on "homotextual space").

5. Richard Henry Dana, *Two Years Before the Mast* (1840; rpt. Garden City, N.Y.: Doubleday, n.d.), p. 153.

6. For a summary account of the captivity narrative as genre, see Roy Harvey Pearce, "The Significance of the Captivity Narrative," *American Literature* 19

(1947): 1–20. More recent work includes Richard Slotkin, *Regeneration Through Violence* (Middletown, Conn.: Wesleyan University Press, 1973).

7. On the captivity theme, see *Typee*, especially p. 243.

8. G. J. Barker-Benfield, *The Horrors of the Half-Known Life: Male Attitudes toward Women and Sexuality in Nineteenth-Century America* (New York: Harper & Row, 1976), p. 12. The 1848 edition of Webster's dictionary, while not referring specifically to masturbation, does make it clear that reverie was used in the mid-nineteenth century as a term with considerable implications of irregularity or even madness: "*Properly*, a raving or delirium; but its sense as generally used is a loose or irregular train of thought, occurring in musing or meditation; wild, extravagant conceit of the fancy or imagination."

9. See Slotkin, *Regeneration Through Violence*, pp. 114 and 125, for theme of cannibalism in Puritan captivity narratives.

10. Barker-Benfield, *Horrors*, p. 173. See also John Todd, *The Young Man: Hints Addressed to the Young Men of the United States* (1844; 4th ed., Northampton: Hopkins, Bridgman & Co., 1850), p. 141.

11. Quoted by Ray B. Browne, *Melville's Drive to Humanism* (Lafayette, Ind.: Purdue University Studies, 1972), p. 83.

12. W. H. Auden, *The Enchafèd Flood; or the Romantic Iconography of the Sea* (1950; rpt. New York: Vintage, 1967), p. 20.

13. Paul Witherington, "The Art of Melville's *Typee*," *Arizona Quarterly* 26 (1970): 137. Cannibalism is an appropriate trope for fellatio, of course.

14. Charles R. Anderson, *Melville in the South Seas* (1939; rpt. New York: Dover, 1966), pp. 132 and 177–78.

15. Milton R. Stern, *The Fine Hammered Steel of Herman Melville* (Urbana: University of Illinois Press, 1968), p. 65.

16. Ibid., p. 248.

17. E. H. Miller, *Melville*, p. 130.

18. Now in the New York Public Library, and quoted with its permission.

19. David Ketterer, "Censorship and Symbolism in *Typee*," *Melville Society Extracts* 34 (1978): 8. See also Gerard M. Sweeney, "Melville's Smoky Humor: Fire-Lighting in *Typee*," *Arizona Quarterly* 34 (1978): 371–76.

20. Anderson, *Melville in the South Seas*, p. 113.

21. A recent article (Mitchell Breitweiser, "False Sympathy in Melville's *Typee*," *American Quarterly* 34 [Fall 1982]: 396–417) claims that "Melville deliberately made his narrator's sympathy eccentric, muddled, and indecisive, and by so doing obliged us to look for the self-interest underlying it" (p. 396). Although much of what he says about Tommo is accurate, and although it is true that the vision of Typee is always filtered through American lenses, nothing in his article demonstrates Melville's relationship to his narrator. Given Melville's subsequent references to Polynesia, this argument is dubious.

22. James Baldwin, *Giovanni's Room* (1956; rpt. New York: Signet, 1959), p. 9.

Chapter 2

1. For the significance of this shift to Romanticism in general, see Harold Bloom, "The Internalization of Quest Romance," in *The Ringers in the Tower: Studies in Romantic Tradition* (Chicago: University of Chicago Press, 1971), pp. 13–35. I do not see the poet as so thoroughly divorced from the world of experience as Bloom does.

2. The English edition of the novel was published in two volumes, the present chapters 1–31 and 32–62. Whether this was Melville's intention is not certain. In any case the novel falls into two parts easily because of its two cities and two journeys. For some of the symbolic patterns of duality in the novel, see Terrence G. Lish, "Melville's *Redburn*: A Study in Dualism," *English Language Notes* 5 (December 1967): 113–20.

3. In biographical terms, Wellingborough may echo Herman Melville's brother's name, Gansevoort, another distinguished family name perhaps inflicted on a young man who would rather have been called Tom or Harry. In both cases the contrast is between European/American, or aristocratic/simple.

4. The echo of the metaphorical contrast of Shakespeare's Sonnet 97 heightens the passage's elegiac tone.

5. See Gerald Monsman, *Walter Pater* (Boston: Twayne, 1977), pp. 30–31.

6. Newton Arvin, *Herman Melville* (New York: William Sloane, 1950), p. 45.

7. Later in the novel, Melville criticizes the "tribal" attitudes of Jews and the concept of an "exclusive" nation. Thus the Jewish characters are deliberate anti-democratic figures.

8. See Michael Davitt Bell's very good commentary in "Melville's *Redburn*: Initiation and Authority," *New England Quarterly* 46 (December 1973): 558–72. Bell argues that the novel illustrates "a shocking and finally enervating realization of the social evil behind or beneath [the] authority [of the fathers]" (p. 561).

9. Jackson's political career was largely based on his defeat of the Creek Indians, which, in the affectless voice of the *Encyclopedia Britannica*, "was so decisive that the Creeks never again were a menace to the frontier, and Jackson was able to impose upon them a treaty whereby they surrendered to the federal government an estimated 23,000,000 acres of land, comprising about one-fifth of the state of Georgia and more than three-fifths of the present state of Alabama. The campaign against the Creeks thus opened a vast new area for settlement and established Jackson as the hero of the west." Jackson's destruction of the Indian nation in the name of (white, English) national expansion is a crucial part of the drive of "civilization" against the "primitive."

10. Jonathan Ned Katz, "Melville's Secret Sex Text," *Village Voice Literary Supplement*, April 1982, p. 11. "Yard" is used specifically for the whale's penis in a text Melville probably knew and used for *Moby-Dick*. Friedrich Martens, "Voyage to Spitzbergen," reprinted in Adam White, ed., *A Collection of Documents on Spitzbergen and Greenland* (London: Hakluyt Society, 1855), p. 110.

11. See my *The Homosexual Tradition in American Poetry* (Austin and London: University of Texas Press, 1979), pp. 21–22, 33–47.

12. Useful correctives to the antidemocratic view of Melville are provided by Charles H. Foster, "Something in Emblems: A Reinterpretation of *Moby-Dick*," *New England Quarterly* 34 (March 1961): 3–35, and Larzer Ziff, "*Moby-Dick* and the Problem of Democratic Literature," *Yearbook of English Studies* 8 (1978): 67–76.

13. It is precisely Melville's intense sense of disappointment at the failure of the democratic (and friendship) ideal that creates his anger at the fallen world.

14. The best recent discussion of the motif, although brief, may be found in Robert Rosenblum, *Modern Painting and the Northern Romantic Tradition: Friedrich to Rothko* (New York: Harper & Row, 1975), pp. 37–40.

15. Hershel Parker, Historical Note to *Redburn*, pp. 331–32.

16. On the pictures, see William H. Gilman, *Melville's Early Life and "Redburn"* (New York: New York University Press, 1951), p. 224 and p. 355 n. 31, and Douglas Robillard, "A Possible Source for Melville's Goetic and Theurgic Magic," *Melville Society Extracts*, no. 49 (February 1982): 5–6. Robillard suggests that the Pompeian reference comes from Bulwer-Lytton's *Last Days of Pompeii*. The depiction of "a most unnatural service," as Gilman puts it, is identified by Harold Beaver in his edition of *Redburn* (Harmondsworth: Penguin, 1976) as fellatio (p. 438).

17. Cf. William B. Dillingham's sneering comment, "It is not at all clear that Melville wanted to depict him as a sexual deviate, although many signs point in that direction. At any rate, mystery prevails in every aspect of his characterization from his background to his hormones." (*An Artist in the Rigging: The Early Work of Herman Melville* [Athens: University of Georgia Press, 1972], p. 42.)

18. Ovid, *Metamorphoses*, trans. Horace Gregory (New York: Mentor, 1960), bk. 10, p. 276: "he taught the men of Thrace the art / of making love to boys."

19. Herbert Marcuse, *Eros and Civilization: A Philosophical Inquiry into Freud* (New York: Vintage, n.d.), pp. 146–51.

20. Amitai Avi-Ram, "Towards a Theory of the Pastoral: The Classics, Walt Whitman, and Hart Crane," Ph.D. diss., Yale University, 1984, p. 155. Avi-Ram's is the most stimulating work on the pastoral that I know of.

21. Forster's remark, from a personal memorandum of 1935, is quoted by Oliver Stallybrass in his introduction to E. M. Forster, *The Life to Come* (London: Edward Arnold, 1972), p. xiv. For J. R. Ackerley, see his *My Father and Myself* (1968; rpt. Harmondsworth: Penguin, 1971).

22. [Frederick Hardman], "Across the Atlantic," *Blackwood's Edinburgh Magazine* 66 (November 1849): 575, 576, 579. See also the anonymous review in *Holden's Dollar Magazine* 5 (January 1850): 55, and the essay on Melville in the *London New Monthly Magazine* 98 (July 1853): 306.

23. Martin Leonard Pops, *The Melville Archetype* (Kent, Ohio: Kent State University Press, 1970), p. 54. Pops bases his reading on the psychoanalytic views of Henry A. Murray. At the same time, Pops identifies Carlo with a "pure autoeroticism." On this point, he seems to me correct.

24. Walter Pater, *The Renaissance: Studies in Art and Poetry* (1873; 1893 text rpt. Berkeley: University of California Press, 1980), pp. 105–9.

25. James E. Miller, Jr., *"Redburn* and *White-Jacket*: Initiation and Baptism," *Nineteenth-Century Fiction* 13 (March 1959): 279.

26. H. Bruce Franklin, "Redburn's Wicked End," *Nineteenth-Century Fiction* 20 (September 1965): 191.

27. Kathleen E. Kier, "An Annotated Edition of Melville's *White-Jacket*," Ph.D. diss., Columbia University, 1980, abstract. Kier's work is extremely valuable. Her study of the allusions in *White-Jacket* shows how a pattern of references to "the names and acts of despotic rulers" underlines Melville's call for "vigilance" against a similar loss of liberty.

28. Ibid., p. 14.

29. See my *The Homosexual Tradition*, pp. 80–82.

30. Precisely what is meant by this term is hard to know. Melville's use of "chum" is consistent with the definition in the 1848 edition of Webster's dictionary ("A chamber-fellow; one who lodges or resides in the same room; *a word used in colleges*"), but he appears to be extending its meaning. Webster does not give the diminutive *chummy* that Melville uses here and in *Mardi*. Later in the century Charles Warren Stoddard, admirer of Whitman's "Calamus" and traveler to the South Seas, would title one of his accounts of a *tayo*-like relationship "Chumming with a Savage." It is interesting to note that Melville also uses the phrase "particular friend" to describe the relation between Jack Chase and White-Jacket; it would seem to echo the French phrase, "amitié particulière."

31. Arvin, *Herman Melville*, p. 128. The sexual allusion to "Rogers's best cutlery" is repeated in *Moby-Dick*, where the overt phallicism creates comic fear in Ishmael.

32. On penetration, see Edward Coke, *The Third Part of the Institute of the Laws of England* (London, 1644), chap. 10, pp. 58–59, cited by Jonathan Katz in *Gay/Lesbian Almanac* (New York: Harper & Row, 1983), p. 89. Penetration was apparently still an issue in the trial of Oscar Wilde (1895), although the legal distinction had ended in 1885.

33. John D. Seelye, "'Spontaneous Impress of Truth': Melville's Jack Chase: A Source, an Analogue, a Conjecture," *Nineteenth-Century Fiction* 20 (March 1966): 372–73.

34. For a forceful presentation of a more negative view of Jack as a "dismal failure," see Yvonne M. Klein, "The Politics of the American Military Novel, 1850–1950," Ph.D. diss., University of Minnesota, 1969.

35. Miller, *"Redburn* and *White-Jacket*," p. 289.

36. The episode is even bleaker about the possibility of resistance to injustice if one bears in mind Melville's apparent source for the episode, the case of Joseph Parker who was jailed for a year in Fitchburg, Massachusetts, in 1830, for refusing to cut his beard (see Howard P. Vincent, *The Tailoring of Melville's "White-Jacket"* [Evanston, Ill.: Northwestern University Press, 1970], pp. 185–86).

37. "Spliced" had already acquired its meaning of "married." The *Oxford English Dictionary* cites two sources Melville certainly knew: Smollett's *Peregrine Pickle* (1751) and Marryat's *Peter Simple* (1834). Melville draws attention to the term in *Moby-Dick* (p. 83).

Chapter 3

1. An effect achieved, of course, by Tom Stoppard.

2. Among the critics who see the Ishmael narrative as central to the novel, I would cite Walter E. Bezanson, *"Moby-Dick:* Work of Art," and Henry Nash Smith, "The Image of Society in *Moby-Dick,"* both in *"Moby-Dick" Centennial Essays,* ed. Tyrus Hillway and Luther S. Mansfield (Dallas: Southern Methodist University Press, 1953), pp. 30–58 and 59–75 respectively; David H. Hirsch, "The Dilemma of the Liberal Intellectual," *Texas Studies in Language and Literature* 5 (Summer 1963): 169–88; James E. Miller, Jr., "Hawthorne and Melville: The Unpardonable Sin," *PMLA* 70 (March 1958): 91–114; and Leslie Fiedler, "Ishmael's Trip," *The Listener,* August 3, 1967, pp. 134–36. For another view of the double plot, see Richard H. Brodhead, *Hawthorne, Melville, and the Novel* (Chicago: University of Chicago Press, 1976), p. 15.

3. C. N. Stavrou, "Ahab and Dick Again," *Texas Studies in Language and Literature* 3 (Autumn 1961): 311, 313.

4. *Culture and Anarchy.*

5. Herbert Marcuse, *Eros and Civilization: A Philosophical Inquiry into Freud* (New York: Vintage, n.d.), pp. 146–56.

6. He acquired a copy of Ovid as part of the Harper's Classical Library in March 1849 (Merton M. Sealts, Jr., *Melville's Reading: A Check-List of Books Owned and Borrowed* [Madison: University of Wisconsin Press, 1966], no. 147). *White-Jacket* was written in the summer of 1849. Gerard M. Sweeney, in "Melville's Use of Classical Mythology," Ph.D. diss., University of Wisconsin, 1972, argues that Melville took his version of Narcissus from Plotinus as well as from Ovid (pp. 305–6, n. 17). Plotinus opposes the search for the beautiful within the self and the desire to grasp "these lower beauties."

7. See especially Leo Marx, *The Machine in the Garden: Technology and the Pastoral Ideal in America* (New York: Oxford University Press, 1964).

8. Melville's English publishers were sufficiently concerned to delete most of the "marriage" references—the reference to a "matrimonial" hug in chapter 4, to "our hearts' honeymoon" in chapter 10, and to Queequeg's "affectionately throwing his brown tattooed legs over mine" in chapter 11. These changes would seem to indicate that they saw the homosexual implications of these passages. Reviewers were generally not offended (of course English reviewers saw only the censored text), although they did complain again about the "rhapsodic" tone. Only the *Methodist Quarterly Review* denounced the "vulgar immoralities that render it unfit for general circulation," without specifying what they were (34 [January 1852]: 154). Many Christian reviewers were offended by Ishmael's "worship" of the idol in chapter 10. They may have seen the Ishmael-Queequeg relationship as a "romantic friendship."

9. Several critics view the marriage as a failure. Martin Pops writes, "Consciously aware of the desirability of marriage and a wife . . . but, at least in part, unconsciously desirous of infantilism and death . . . , Ishmael is driven between these extremes to his homoerotic compromise. Therefore, although he is saved by

Eros . . . and although his love for Queequeg is creative and convincing, his is, from the ontogenetic point of view, a compromised sexuality nonetheless" (*The Melville Archetype* [Kent, Ohio: Kent State University Press, 1970], p. 82). Beneath the jargon, the argument is that, although Melville saw the marriage of Ishmael and Queequeg as the means of Ishmael's redemption, we know better, since homosexual relationships represent a "compromise." More recently, Sharon Cameron has argued that the marriage is an escape: "the power of the homosexual relationship lies in the discrepancy between its representation of transport—its life-saving gift—and its exemption from the turmoil of ordinary life. Much of what endears Queequeg to us, as to Ishmael, is the way he fulfills an unspeakable fantasy in which a mystical partner makes the ultimate sacrifice, sullying neither it nor himself in the world's banalities" (*The Corporeal Self: Allegories of the Body in Melville and Hawthorne* [Baltimore: Johns Hopkins University Press, 1981], pp. 42–43). Cameron's own views of homosexuality seem to intrude themselves between her and the text: it is obvious that Queequeg regularly "sullies himself" in "ordinary life"; it is precisely his role to pull Ishmael from solipsism to involvement, through their love.

10. Robert Shulman, "The Serious Function of Melville's Phallic Jokes," *American Literature* 33 (May 1961): 186. Shulman also identifies the whale with a threatening phallic energy, whereas I find the whale to be clearly bisexual, as antedating sexual division. Important in recognizing Melville's project to restore a reclaimed phallicism is his omission of the ordinary, Aristotelian Greek word for whale ($\phi\acute{\alpha}\lambda\lambda\alpha\iota\nu\alpha$) from the Etymology. Without the "λ," as Melville hints, the phallus becomes the whale (Latin *balaena*). The claim of descent from $\chi\eta\tau o\varsigma$ is an act of evasion that calls attention to the absent origin.

It is perhaps worth noting that Americans of the nineteenth century generally did not see Indians in terms of sexual threat—although they saw blacks that way. (See Michael Paul Rogin, *Fathers and Children: Andrew Jackson and the Subjugation of the American Indian* [New York: Knopf, 1975] p. 125.) However, I think it is likely that the Indian was perceived as a *homosexual* threat: homosexuality and cross-dressing were well known among Indians, and public rhetoric referred to Indians in terms of sterility and small cocks. Because Indians lacked private property, they were thought of as lacking a strong ego; and both property and ego are identified with male heterosexual behavior. When Ishmael sleeps with Queequeg, he returns in his memory to a childhood scene of punishment (for masturbation?); to sleep with an Indian means to abandon one's white male adulthood for childishness and lack of will; whereas to sleep with a black would indicate the abandonment of reason for lust. Blacks are stereotyped in American legend as the rapists of women, while Indians are stereotyped as the lovers of men.

11. This is noted by Harold Beaver in his edition of *Moby-Dick* (Harmondsworth: Penguin, 1972). Although Beaver's overzealous editing is often ludicrous, he seems to be right on this point. He does not view the sperm-squeezing episode favorably, despite seeing homosexual references everywhere in the novel, but instead as the "ultimate illusion" (p. 876). For a very different interpretation of the significance of Yojo's name, see David H. Hirsch, "Verbal Reverberation and the

Problem of Reality in *Moby-Dick*," *Books at Brown* 24 (1971): 45–67. Hirsch sees Yojo as a version of the tetragrammaton and a sign of the idol's "real" religious significance. This is not inconsistent with my view that Yojo is a phallic god.

12. Marx, *The Machine in the Garden*, pp. 304–9.

13. See my *The Homosexual Tradition in American Poetry* (Austin and London: University of Texas Press, 1979), pp. 19–22.

14. Roland Barthes, *Le plaisir du texte* (Paris: Le Seuil, 1973), p. 10.

15. Roland Barthes, *S/Z* (1970; rpt. Paris: Le Seuil, 1976), p. 19.

16. On Ahab's links to Prometheus, see Richard Chase, *Herman Melville: A Critical Study* (New York: Macmillan, 1954), and H. Bruce Franklin, *The Wake of the Gods: Melville's Mythology* (Stanford: Stanford University Press, 1963).

17. In an excellent analysis, Stephen C. Ausband writes that Ahab's isolation is due to what he calls misophuism, or "hatred of the natural. A machine is the perfect metaphor to describe Ahab's force, and only in the opposition of the mechanical to the natural could Melville have pictured so powerfully and so perfectly a man waging relentless, mindless war on the essence of life." ("The Whale and the Machine: An Approach to *Moby-Dick*," *American Literature* 47 [May 1975]: 211.) Melville's most memorable depiction of the mechanical/masculine forces and their relationship to nature is of course "The Tartarus of Maids."

18. Tony Tanner, *City of Words: American Fiction 1950–1970* (London: Jonathan Cape, 1976), p. 22.

19. John Updike, *The Centaur* (New York: Knopf, 1963), p. 293.

20. James B. Hall, "*Moby-Dick*: Parable of a Dying System," *Western Review* 14 (Spring 1950): 223–26.

21. Alan Heimert, "*Moby-Dick* and American Political Symbolism," *American Quarterly* 15 (Winter 1963): 498–534. The essay concludes that Melville was one of very few observers of his time who were able to realize "that the Compromise of 1850 represented, in essence, a victory for an economic entente, an outgrowth of the Industrial Revolution, which needed peace in order to preserve and enhance its status."

22. Similarly, in "Benito Cereno" the skeleton of the slave owner, Don Alexandro, replaces the figurehead of Columbus, signaling the racial crimes at the origin of Western history in the New World.

23. In *Pierre*, Melville's next novel, the ancestral estate is built by the family of a victorious Indian fighter on land that had belonged to the Indians. Like Faulkner later, Melville sees American history built on a foundation of theft and genocide. That political realization is the equivalent of the personal realization of Pierre's father's illegitimate daughter: each is a crime that destroys any possibility of preserving faith in the inherited order.

24. Hershel Parker plays down the importance of Shaw for Melville and claims that "*Moby-Dick* was too nearly finished to have been much affected by whatever he may have learned about the fugitive slave cases [from Shaw in July 1851]." "Melville and Politics: A Scrutiny of the Political Milieux of Herman Melville's Life and Works," Ph.D. diss., Northwestern University, 1963, p. 202. Since the references are all in a single chapter, there is no reason why they could not have

been added at a late date in the composition. Parker consistently argues against the "political" element in Melville, but he usually has a very narrow definition of politics. The case for the importance of Shaw's decision in the Sims case for Melville's composition of *Moby-Dick* was first made by Charles Foster, but he does not discuss the "Fast Fish and Loose Fish" chapter.

25. Harrison Hayford, "Unnecessary Duplicates: A Key to the Writing of *Moby-Dick*," in Faith Pullin, ed., *New Perspectives on Melville* (Edinburgh: University of Edinburgh Press, 1978), pp. 128–61. Hayford suggests a stage in which Bulkington was to be the narrator's comrade; this role of Bulkington's was then assigned to Queequeg, while Bulkington's role as Romantic hero was given to Ahab.

26. Smith, "Image of Society in *Moby-Dick*," p. 75.

27. Some of the parallels to the Fisher King story are pointed out in a not very interesting essay by Janet Dow, "Ahab: The Fisher King," *Connecticut Review* 2 (April 1965): 42–49.

28. See particularly chapter 95, with its reference, in a clearly phallic context, to "the secret groves of Queen Maachah in Judea" and her dethronement by her son, a paradigm of the imposition of patriarchal rule, and the discussion of this passage above, p. 83.

Chapter 4

1. Edwin Haviland Miller, *Melville* (New York: George Braziller, 1975), pp. 249–50.

2. Nathaniel Hawthorne, *The House of the Seven Gables*, Centenary Edition, vol. 2 (Columbus: Ohio State University Press, 1965), pp. 31–32.

3. Nathaniel Hawthorne, *The Marble Faun: or, The Romance of Monte Beni*, Centenary Edition, vol. 4 (Columbus: Ohio State University Press, 1968), p. 285.

4. I accidentally came across a striking confirmation of this point. Kathleen Kier, explaining the sexual allusion in *White-Jacket* in the phrase "the rule of three," quotes a wonderfully salacious letter from Benjamin Franklin to Catherine Ray in 1755: "I hope you will become an expert in the *Rule of Three*; that when I have again the pleasure of seeing you, I may find you like my Grape Vine, surrounded with Clusters, plump, juicy, blushing, pretty little rogues, like their Mamma" (quoted in "An Annotated Edition of Melville's *White Jacket*" [Ph.D. diss., Columbia University], p. 107, from Benjamin Franklin, *Representative Selections*, ed. Chester Jorgenson and Frank L. Mott [rev. ed., New York: Hill and Wang, 1962], p. 277).

5. There is a considerable body of literature on the literary consequences of the Hawthorne-Melville relationship and their subsequent estrangement. On *The Blithedale Romance*, see Henry A. Murray, ed., *Pierre* (New York: Hendricks House, 1949), pp. lxxv–lxxix; Edward G. Lueders, "The Melville-Hawthorne Relationship in *Pierre* and *The Blithedale Romance*," *Western Humanities Review* 4

(Autumn 1950): 323–34; and, more recently, Charles N. Watson, Jr., "The Estrangement of Hawthorne and Melville," *New England Quarterly* 46 (September 1973): 380–402. Watson's analysis of a pattern of overture and rebuff is convincing, although his comments on *The Marble Faun* surprisingly restrict themselves to the Kenyon/Miriam relationship.

6. The link to *The Symposium* is made by Walter Sutton, "Melville's 'Pleasure Party' and the Art of Concealment," *Philological Quarterly* 30 (July 1951): 316–27. Sutton sees Melville's use of techniques of concealment as the result of "the necessity of dealing indirectly . . . with subjects which were socially unacceptable" and asserts that "Melville was fully aware of the bisexual implications of the poem." He does not develop the significance of the Hawthorne reference. Whatever the actual date of this poem, it is certainly one of the first modern works to explicitly defend homosexuality or bisexuality, and its use of *Urania* strikingly anticipates the Uranian poets of the turn of the century. It is virtually impossible that Melville would have known of them.

7. W. H. Auden, *The Enchafèd Flood; or the Romantic Iconography of the Sea* (1950; rpt. New York: Vintage, 1967), p. 146n.

8. See F. Barron Freeman, ed., *Melville's "Billy Budd"* (Cambridge: Harvard University Press, 1948), Appendix 1, 2, p. [356].

9. Cf. Melville's comment in "Benito Cereno" that the "perverse habit" of "hard self-restraint" transforms man into "a loaded cannon" (pp. 63–64).

10. Herman Melville, *Journal of a Visit to Europe and the Levant October 11, 1856-May 6, 1857*, ed. Howard C. Horsford (Princeton: Princeton University Press, 1955), entry for February 25 [1857], p. 191.

11. The choice among three unsatisfactory possibilities was already employed by Melville as the structure of "Benito Cereno," where civilized decadence, primitive violence, and American "innocence" interact.

12. Milton R. Stern, *The Fine Hammered Steel of Herman Melville* (Urbana: University of Illinois Press, 1957), p. 27.

13. C. N. Manlove, "An Organic Hesitancy: Theme and Style in *Billy Budd*," in Faith Pullin, ed., *New Perspectives on Melville* (Edinburgh: Edinburgh University Press, 1978), p. 280.

14. Leonard Casper, "The Case against Captain Vere," *Perspective* 5 (Summer 1952): 150.

15. Wendell Glick, "Expediency and Absolute Morality in *Billy Budd*," *PMLA* 68 (March 1953): 104.

16. Ibid., p. 105.

17. Ibid., p. 109; Ralph W. Willett, "Nelson and Vere: Hero and Victim in *Billy Budd, Sailor*," *PMLA* 82 (October 1967): 370.

18. Mary Foley, "The Digressions in *Billy Budd*," in William T. Stafford, ed., *Melville's "Billy Budd" and the Critics* (San Francisco: Wadsworth Publishing Co., 1961), p. 163.

19. Richard T. Stavig, "Melville's *Billy Budd*: A New Approach to the Problem of Interpretation," Ph.D. diss., Princeton University, 1953, p. 70. This work,

which focuses on the use Melville makes of the *Somers* mutiny, is still extremely valuable; it should have been published years ago. I should perhaps record Stavig's disagreement with me on one important point: he thinks the claim that Claggart has homosexual impulses is "unwarranted speculation" (p. 205, n. 119).

20. The most consistent defender of Vere and Melville's belief in the "forms" is Milton R. Stern. In the introduction to his edition of *Billy Budd* (Indianapolis: Bobbs-Merrill, 1975), he uses the poem to justify his defense of Vere. Why the Civil War poems (his principal evidence) should be privileged over the fiction or the later poems (let alone the text of *Billy*) as an indication of Melville's intentions is not clear. But even the poems Stern cites do not so clearly demonstrate what he claims for them. The nostalgia for the more "glorious" wars of the past is attributed to "an Englishman of the old order," whereas the "utilitarian view" is that war is "now placed— / Where war belongs— / Among the trades and artisans." The poems are more concerned with the loss of life on both sides than with a romantic presentation of war. Even Melville's apparent defense of "time and measure perfect" must be examined in the light of his actual poetic practice. It is clear that Melville feared the effects of the mob and that he saw that society's need to put down the mob during the draft riots violated the spirit of "the Republic's faith." But this recognition is one of despair, not celebration. In *Billy Budd*, it should be recalled, there are no mobs, but the power prompted by the fear of mobs remains. In defense of society the Claggarts are allowed to triumph. That seems to me the insight Melville draws from history.

21. Foley, "Digressions in *Billy Budd*," p. 162.

22. The *Oxford English Dictionary* gives the earliest use of the modern sense as 1869.

23. Ray B. West, Jr., "The Unity of *Billy Budd*," *Hudson Review* 5 (Spring 1952): 127.

24. Ray B. Browne, "*Billy Budd*: Gospel of Democracy," *Nineteenth-Century Fiction* 17 (March 1963): 337.

25. Karl E. Zink, "Herman Melville and the Forms—Irony and Social Criticism in 'Billy Budd'," *Accent* 12 (Summer 1952): 139.

26. I allude here, of course, to the two famous poles of *Billy Budd* criticism, embodied in two essays: E. L. Grant Watson, "Melville's Testament of Acceptance," *New England Quarterly* 6 (June 1933): 319–27; and Phil Withim, "*Billy Budd*: Testament of Resistance," *Modern Language Quarterly* 20 (June 1959): 115–27. The problem with most *Billy Budd* criticism is its implicit assumption that either Billy or Vere must be the hero and a consequent tendency to take remarks about one or the other of them ironically; but no one seems to have recognized that Melville is ironic about both of them.

27. If he had had to choose, he would have chosen Billy, I believe. But a choice between unacceptable alternatives is not much of a choice.

28. Barbara Johnson, "Melville's Fist: The Execution of *Billy Budd*," *Studies in Romanticism* 18 (Winter 1979): 569.

29. On the influence of Schopenhauer, see Walter Sutton, "Melville and the

Great God Budd," *Prairie Schooner* 34 (Summer 1960): 128–33, and Olive Fite, "Billy Budd, Claggart, and Schopenhauer," *Nineteenth-Century Fiction* 23 (1968): 336–43.

30. Irving Howe, "Anarchy and Authority in American Literature," *Denver Quarterly* 2 (Autumn 1967): 27.

Index

~~~~~~